Love Me,
Love My Kids

LOVE ME, LOVE MY KIDS

A Guide for the New Partner

PETER ROWLANDS

CONTINUUM : NEW YORK

1983

The Continuum Publishing Company
575 Lexington Avenue
New York, New York 10022

Printed in the United States of America

Library of Congress Cataloging in Publication Data

Rowlands, Peter.
Love me, love my kids.

1. Stepmothers—Family relationships. I. Title.
HQ759.92.R68   1983   646.7′8   83-10101
ISBN 0-8264-0239-9

Contents

Foreword

When I wrote *Saturday Parent* in 1979, I concentrated on the problems of the parent who lives apart from his or her children, who does not have custody but wants to make the most of access. During that time I was frequently aware of another person whose behavior and attitudes greatly influenced the success of the attempts to keep up contact and to make it work well for both parent and child. This was a person who often lacked a precise name. Usually, but not always, this was a woman. She was introduced in various ways: "second wife," "friend," "fiancée," and even "this is my common law," or "Here's Naomi—she comes in from time to time and she's a human being I can relate to." "Partner" is, I feel, the best appellation, and this is what I use in this book.

It is you, the new partner, whom I am now addressing. From a large number of interviews, it is obvious that you have quite a task on your hands. You can do a lot of good; and you can become extremely frustrated. You are the one who has to respond when you realize that your partner is telling you—even if not in so many words—"Love me, love my kids."

Among the statistics I unearthed for *Saturday Parent* was the calculation that in the United States the proportion of homes with children where there was only one parent in residence (either because of an official or an unofficial split) was approximately two in seven. In Canada the proportion was one in four. Since then, both these figures have changed.

Divorce Rate and One-Parent Families

	Divorce Rate		Percentage of One-Parent Families	
	1978	*1983*	*1978*	*1983*
USA	30%	35%	27%	29%
CANADA	28%	32%	24%	26%

Various factors, notably remarriage, combine to keep the level of one-parent families below the level of the divorce rate. But the continued growth of one-parent families points to the continuing relevance of the Saturday parent. This in turn makes it important to look at what new partners feel about Saturday parenting, and how this affects the results.

As the new partner of a Saturday parent, you have very considerable social significance nowadays. And yet you are not often recognized as existing, let alone important. Your time has come.

Saturday parents are more visible all the time. Nowadays people are far less likely to lock themselves into cupboards after there is a marriage breakdown. Nor is there the requirement now, as there used to be in most American social groups, for a full-scale commitment (that is, remarriage) before a new partnership gets established. Therefore, new partners like yourself are also more likely to enter the scene more quickly.

However, you are still liable to be suspect, regardless of whether you had anything to do with the marriage breakup. Your influence on a child is sometimes assumed to be "disturbing"; sometimes it is dismissed as "inconsequential." It is difficult to see how it can be *both* of these at the same time. And if I have learned anything from the interviews I have conducted, it is that generalizing is pointless. You can disturb a child if you really try, and few want to do that. But you are in a position to be extremely helpful to a child, and to your partner as well. It is up to you.

The idea of calling you Mrs. Saturday Parent appealed to me at first. But this is a bit fanciful, and it sounds as if someone is forcing the pace too quickly. You may be in the process of deciding whether that role appeals to you. Nowadays, many test the water before they jump in.

Read what is said about meeting your partner's children before you commit yourself even to the dipping of a toe. Children are not incidentals. Even on the basis of occasional visits, they will be a very salient part of your relationship. Even if you have a child of your own, adding a visiting child to a resident child (or to another visiting child) is not as straightforward as it might seem.

There are some apologies I should make. The first is for addressing you as a female (except in chapter 10, which specifically talks to the new male partner). In doing so I am simply following the statistical likelihood and making the book easier to read.

The second apology is for making "the child" in this book a "he." I refuse to call a child "it." And the sheer number of references to children makes the alternatives of always using the plural form or saying "the young person" seem really clumsy and intimidating. However, when I *emphasize* the possibility that a boy *or* a girl might be involved, I use "he or she."

Many intricate family groupings and regroupings are allowed for in this book. But certain people are bound to be disappointed. There has been neither sufficient material nor space, for example, to include sections on multiple previous marriages, commune arrangements, or cases where the new partnership is homosexual. These are areas for more specific research.

Once again I want to thank profusely all these people who consented to give interviews to help prepare the ground. These included new partners, Saturday parents, some custodial parents, and some children. As far as I could I have changed details in order to protect their anonymity without deviating from the points they made.

I thank my wife, Susi, for sowing the first seed of the book, for hitting on an ingenious title, and for helping me throughout.

1 : "What a Way to Spend Saturday Afternoon!"

There is always a danger in approaching a particular child as a special child, with a special problem, to the extent of forgetting that basically he is just a *child*. There are a lot of characteristics that children share. Don't assume that a child is extraordinary until he proves himself so.

A quick catch-up on children

There are twenty points to remember where children are concerned; these points apply whatever the circumstances. Forget for a moment where your partner's child is coming from and why. If you can bear in mind the points summarized below, and act on them, a lot of the basics will be right.

Children detest

1. being laughed at. Laugh *with* them by all means, but remember that even an infant knows when he is being laughed at.
2. being referred to as "he" or "she" in their presence, as if they were chairs or pictures, unable to join in the conversation.
3. being promised something, and then being let down, especially "I'll call you next weekend," or "I'll see you soon." Their memories for this are long.
4. having either of their parents criticized in front of them.
5. being made to "perform" in front of unknown people (singing,

1

reciting, whatever). If they want to perform, you will know all about it.

6. being cooped up for any length of time on "best behavior," without any opportunity to relax or to release energy.
7. changing the rules for one's own benefit, or to suit other children.
8. personal remarks, particularly in front of others, from "my, how you've grown" to "your hair needs cutting."
9. being separated for too long from a brother or a sister of the same age or older.
10. being forced to make a choice when they are too young to understand the alternatives.

Children appreciate

11. knowing what to call you: your first name is the easiest, the most natural, the least embarrassing, and the best.
12. being asked what they like to eat and drink, and what they dislike.
13. a change in routine, new ideas about where to go and what to do—provided this does not threaten their basic pattern of meeting important needs.
14. being encouraged to be helpful, provided interesting jobs are rotated with dull ones, and especially if jobs are shared with adults.
15. being asked their opinion about a film, a book, a person . . . anything, so long as you sound as if you are genuinely interested in their view.
16. some space, maybe just a little corner, in which they can be themselves, and to which they can come back to knowing that it is theirs.
17. having their personal property respected.
18. having their confidences respected.
19. getting acquainted slowly, securely.
20. being recognized as an individual, that is being allowed some talent or peculiarity that is not like anyone else's.

What This Book Is About

This book is for you as you wait for the car to come back. Inside it will be the person you love, with whom you are now living. With that person will be somebody you haven't met before—a young child you may have discussed several times, but never actually seen or engaged in conversation.

As you wait for the car you are certainly wondering what this confrontation is going to mean. You will be making contact with a significant part of your lover's life, your lover's child from a marriage that has ended. This is part of your learning about each other. Probably you have already revealed most of the people and things that are important to you. Now it is time for your lover to make a similar revelation.

This is "show and tell" played for very high stakes: is it going to be a foretaste, perhaps, of the kind of child that the two of you might produce together someday? In this meeting you will be provided with a view into the past and a glimpse of a possible future.

The car seems to be taking a long time. Maybe the traffic is heavy downtown on this Saturday afternoon. But there might be a more sinister reason for the delay. At the last moment the child's other parent (the one with custody) may have decided against the whole idea of a visit this week—or *any* week. There may have been a sudden change of mind, the terms of the decree (if any) may simply be ignored. In another part of town there is very likely resentment that this child is coming within your orbit. There may be a last gravitational pull to try to keep the child away from your influence.

It may also be, of course, that this will be an unwilling visitor. Nervousness or fear or anger or any combination of these emotions may get in the way of a friendly response. You cannot be sure, at your distance, about what has or hasn't gone on inside his home. You can smile a friendly smile and watch for signs that will show you whether you are being regarded with an open mind or through a distorting mirror.

All those little anecdotes you have been told about the cute or the dreadful things that the child did at three, five, or fifteen crowd into your mind. You sort through them. But you probably realize that stories like that, even told by a parent, can only give you a very shadowy picture of how this young person is going to seem to *you*.

A lot depends on the kind of preparation you have been going through with your partner. Perhaps you had to use persuasion to get agreement to take this step. Perhaps it was the other way around, in which case you may already be regretting that you gave in. Perhaps it was a spur-of-the-moment decision based on a mutual feeling that the two of you are close enough now to add this dimension to your lives. How far you feel excited or apprehensive or anxious to prove that this was the right thing to do depends on how you arrived at the decision to take this step. But you would be unusual if you were not nervous—unless, of course, you have already played this scene through before, with a different cast.

The aim of this book is to give you some preliminary help. A great number of people have been through your situation. Some of their stories are presented in this book, and their accounts give some helpful ideas about what to try for and what to avoid. They can give you some perspective as you wait for that car that stubbornly refuses to arrive.

Your relationship is different from the classic "second-time-around" marriage. All those books that prepare people to become stepparents (usually after one of the parents has died) are very wide of the mark as far as you are concerned. You are essentially a product of our times: you are not necessarily married, and you may or may not intend to marry sometime. You may be live-in or live-out. You may not regard your relationship as permanent, and you may even be sharing your mate with one or more others. For the sake of simplicity, I am talking to you as if to the most typical person: you are most likely unmarried, but are in a relationship that you feel has potential for at least a long and mutually satisfying time together. You are probably living together. In many cases you will have a child already, but this does not go for the majority. Statistics suggest that you very probably want to have one or more children of your own at some stage, although this, too, varies.

You are more likely to be a woman. But since more men now-adays are getting custody of the children—whether officially or unofficially—this means that you may well be a man who is the new partner of the noncustodial parent. However, since such men are still a relatively small minority, the reader is addressed as a woman from this point on (except in Chapter 10, which has been written specifically with men in mind). However, much of the advice, and most of the case histories are applicable to either sex.

This book will not be able to tell you exactly what kind of child will emerge from the car, but it will give you plenty of ideas about what might be going on in his mind, and why. As the title of the book implies, I am very conscious of the fact that the emotional current running between yourself and your lover is vital. The two of you are relating to each other, not just to the child. The argument of this book is that time and again problems affecting a second partnership or a second marriage have their origins in disagreements about how close you should be getting to the children.

Whatever the background may be, a child is about to enter your life. The following case history may contain elements similar to your own situation.

Charlene

When John, with whom Charlene had recently moved in, at last came home with his four-year-old daughter, Tracy, Charlene ran out to greet them with a broad smile and a cheerful "Hi!"

She got an answer from John, but Tracy virtually ignored her. As Tracy ran past her into the house there was just the merest hint of a glance in Charlene's direction. But it was more as if to avoid running into her than to make contact. For the next couple of hours Tracy concentrated exclusively on her father, who gave her a lot of time because he was anxious to please her. Occasionally Charlene asked Tracy a question like "Would you like to put some clothes on this doll with me?" or "Would you like a chocolate brownie?" Each time Tracy seemed to catch the meaning, but almost unwillingly. She picked up the doll, admired it, pulled at its hair, and put it aside. She grunted, reached for the plate of brownies, and muttered a scarcely audible "thank you" when John asked her for it. But it was as if some robot had been there, not a real person.

"I couldn't say that she disliked me," is Charlene's verdict on this meeting, years after the event. "Like or dislike simply didn't apply. I just was not there. I was an obstacle for her to look around, and I was a brownie vending machine that didn't even ask for quarters. My God, I hated that."

It had taken some time for Tracy's mother to agree to her child meeting up with Charlene at all. The reason given was that this would be too upsetting for Tracy, who was "too confused as it is." Tracy's mother had also declared heatedly that she didn't want her daughter exposed "to a whole series of tramps." Meanwhile, John had been caught in the middle of two opposing forces. He felt his contact with Tracy, whom he loved dearly, was threatened. But he felt that his happiness and his long-term future with Charlene were also threatened if he continued to exclude her from a large portion of his weekend life. This is a fairly common dilemma.

When at last Tracy's mother had agreed to Charlene's meeting Tracy, Charlene thought that everything would surely be better. Instead, Tracy refused to acknowledge Charlene's presence. It was disappointing and frustrating. John was concerned that Charlene shouldn't take offense against his daughter. "Just give her time," he advised.

Charlene tried at first to notice and to remember all she could that would help make Tracy feel at home—the objects she seemed interested in, the chair she preferred to sit on, the treats she enjoyed, her preference for apple juice over orange juice. She provided these things—but they were accepted automatically, as if that was exactly how they *should* be.

She got down on all fours occasionally to be at Tracy's level and to play or read with Tracy. Sometimes this tactic seemed on the verge of success: Tracy would glance over to Charlene in curiosity, and once or twice actually reached to touch what Charlene was holding. But as soon as she sensed that attention was being paid to her, she rapidly slipped out of range.

It didn't help Charlene very much to talk to her friends. Their advice ranged from "Hang in, keep trying to get something going with her" to "Pick her up by the ears and tell her it's time to wise up" to "Butt out and go to a movie instead."

Each Saturday afternoon seemed to be etched in gray. Even when they went out together, the closest she ever got to Tracy was when she took her into the women's washroom. She started to talk to John about this, but she felt irritated when he accused her of exaggerating everything. "Sure she notices you," he insisted. "She likes you."

It took a strange incident to convince Charlene that there might in fact be some truth in this, that she was not simply wasting her own and everyone else's time by staying around on Saturdays.

Charlene suffers from an occasional migraine. It doesn't hit her often, but when it does, her only recourse is to lie down in a darkened room with an ice pack and try to sleep. This happened to her one Saturday. She was half-asleep when she suddenly heard voices at her bedside. John was hissing from the doorway, "Tracy, come back out of there!"

Tracy put her hand on Charlene's shoulder and stared hard at the patient. "Oh boy," she said.

"Hi, Tracy," Charlene managed to say.

"Hi. How are you doing?"

"Okay."

"Take this."

Charlene felt her mouth and nose suddenly covered with fur. Coughing and choking she freed her face from what proved to be a toy monkey. John lifted Tracy up and away, saying he was sorry she'd been disturbed. When she woke up the monkey was still on her pillow.

She just had time to come downstairs and give Tracy a hug and a kiss before John got out the car to take Tracy back. She gave credit to the monkey for a rapid recovery, and tried to give it back.

"Keep it till next time," Tracy advised solemnly. She was returning the hug.

This is not what can be called a typical turning point. From the many case histories that involve such a moment, there are only a few generalizations that can be drawn:

1. A turning point has to be initiated by the child.
2. It often comes when hope of a breakthrough has almost been given up but the parent's partner perseveres nonetheless.
3. It often seems to result from a power-reversal situation, when for some reason the child no longer feels in awe of somebody powerful and gains ascendancy.

This incident happened over eight years ago. Charlene and John are now married. Tracy calls up sometimes and asks if she can come over. There have been difficult times, discipline problems, the occasional shouting match. But for Charlene these are virtually without significance when she considers the enjoyment she has experienced watching and helping Tracy grow up. Equally important has been her feeling that John has been helped to have a very happy relationship with his daughter.

It seems important to Charlene, looking back, that Tracy was a child to whom she felt personally drawn. "Even when she spent all her time avoiding me, I kind of liked her." This is, of course, not always the case.

In the long run, Charlene is one of the luckier people discussed in this book: despite numerous rebuffs she persevered, and she, John, and Tracy have benefited from knowing each other better and giving each other more and more.

While some people may be able to click together from the start, there are others who have nothing but problems. To get a fair picture, they have to be considered, too.

Margaret

Margaret is now in her fifties. She recalls life with David, with whom she had a common-law relationship less than two years back, with some regret. "We had good times," she explains. "But I couldn't stand his kids."

Margaret and David used to argue about whether his two teenage boys by his first marriage (fourteen and fifteen years old) should occupy so much of his, and their, time. She tried to get him to put a distance between themselves and his former life, including the two boys.

At first, she claims, she was completely open-minded. Then, one Sunday afternoon, they arrived. One was "hyper" and the other was sullen. Terry, the hyper boy, was the younger brother. "They looked at me like two unfriendly animals—they should have been behind bars." Margaret is convinced that from the outset neither boy liked her looks, her way of speaking, her relationship with David, or her presence in his house. They didn't smile when they said hello. Instead, they seemed to her to be sizing her up, to see what her weak points might be. "They found them, all right," Margaret recalls bitterly.

During one visit they had a slingshot fight with each other in the backyard. When one broke a window and she protested, they swore at her and called her a fancy cow. During another visit, Terry entertained himself by running from room to room slamming doors. Margaret tried to catch him and stop him. The kitchen door slammed in her face. It broke her nose.

It should have made her suspicious, Margaret says, that their mother was totally in favor of their visiting for long periods—the longer the better, and as often as possible.

The tensions surrounding the boys' visits were a major cause, in her view, of her final breakup with David. He had no intention of giving up on them, although he was sympathetic to how she felt. She found herself disliking the boys more and more, and stopped looking for points of contact. She opted out of the Sunday visits, but this did not stop her from being sad and angry at the chaos she found in the house when she returned.

At no time did these children seem like persons that she would be happy to know. There was absolutely nothing on which to build. Infuriatingly, David agreed that they were almost devoid of redeeming features, but he did nothing to help them improve, or to help her accept them. She could not accept his kind of fatalism.

There is another important theme in this case history. Close to the root of the failure was a profound difference of opinion as to how children should be brought up. He was very lenient, while she was accustomed to children obeying some rules.

Often a report of "dislike from the word go" coincides with complaints about lack of support between the two partners about how to handle the child. From this it is a short step to feeling that the whole enterprise was doomed from the start, that there was always something about the child that one could never really have accepted.

There are other reasons for difficulties between the new partner and the children, but remarkably often they can be linked to a failure in communication between the partners. Take the example of Margaret. David was seemingly able to notice the difference between his own children's behavior and what the majority of parents would like to see as "normal" behavior, yet he was unable to offer any suggestions or take any initiatives toward control or improvement. Although the extent of Margaret's willingness to work at it may be questioned, she seems to have been crying out for some sign from him that they might be aiming jointly at creating harmony with the boys.

No one can expect his new partner *single-handedly* to shoulder the main burdens of planning visits, looking after the children's needs, sorting out quarrels, developing an understanding, and applying discipline. In fact, if you suspect that you are being set up for this role, it makes sense to back off for a little while, decide what it is that *you* want, and then discuss with your partner what you feel is happening, telling him precisely how you yourself see the future.

A surprising number of case histories involve somebody like yourself suddenly realizing that they are being put into the driver's seat. Some rejected the idea. Others felt a kind of responsibility, as if a younger brother or sister had suddenly arrived, and there was nobody taking much notice of them. There are plenty of examples of bonds between a child and a new partner becoming stronger than any others in the immediate neighborhood and surviving long after contact with the natural parents has dwindled.

The potential for a close relationship between you and the child is usually there, provided that the situation doesn't make you feel that you are being exploited. Exploitation can be in the amount of time you are expected to devote to child rearing, or in the level of responsibility that you are suddenly being required to take on. Usually there is a mixture of these two aspects.

There is some truth in the saying that most martyrs are self-made. I prefer to believe that only a minority of the readers of this book will create their own exploitation to use as an emotional weapon. When exploitation does occur, most people have had it thrust upon them.

It is very hard to see the good side of a child when you are feeling bad about the way that his visits are robbing your weekends of relaxation and of the chance to enjoy adult activities or quiet moments with your partner. It is important from the start to be aware of how much of the organization, how much of the problem solving, and how much of the sheer time involved is being left to you. The sooner you open up the discussion about any imbalance with your partner the better. Leaving it for a few weeks "to see how the pattern settles down" may be fatal. By this time your partner may persuade himself that you *enjoy* changing the diapers while he gets in a quick round of golf. When your resentment finally bursts its banks, he may be puzzled, and he will even suggest it's your own fault.

The time is the 1980s, a time when both sexes understand more readily that looking after children is an experience to share. There is no point in leaping in with recriminations. Just state your feelings and negotiate. When fathers say good-bye to their children after a visit, many partners find that they are on a downswing. You have to find ways of breaking through this, without making your partner feel that he is being interrogated. Picking up on children's comments is as good a way as any of getting the conversation going more easily: "He said he didn't like the dog much. What do you think he meant?" You can then swing the conversation on to how future visits might be organized, giving vent to any feelings of exploitation you might have.

So far as can be determined from a secondhand account, Margaret's partner had a rather severe case of prolonged guilt. He was no longer anxious to try to help improve his sons' behavior and get a more positive spirit into their weekend meetings. He had despaired, and in his own way he was enjoying the despair. In addition to the straightforward exploitation that Margaret was expected to endure, she had the problem of his guilt to contend with, too. She was, and is, a positive person. The guilty fatalism was more than she could stand, and the love between her and David could not stand it either.

The justification for including Margaret and David's case study is that the existence of failures has to be acknowledged, and that analyzing what happened there can be very helpful in showing what to watch out for and what to avoid.

Success in this kind of relationship is a measure of the frequency with which things go well and of the degree to which the good side makes the bad side seem unimportant. Perfect alignment between yourself and somebody else's children is simply not to be expected. Refusing to believe that anything can go seriously wrong, that you will draw close to each other very rapidly and without hesitations, is a frame of mind that seems to increase the likelihood of problems. Curiously, those who start with maximum optimism are at as much of a disadvantage as those who are very pessimistic. The overly optimistic tend to start with a romantic delusion of being able to create by sheer enthusiasm the perfect nuclear family from the material that suddenly comes to hand. Not so—or very rarely. It needs working on, not just a strong intention. They are not allowing for the individuality of the child, for the fact that at whatever age he or she might be, there is an individual personality that has its own set of experiences, hopes, and fears. This child is a person, not just malleable material. When you get to know this person, and when you in turn are better understood, then the two of you will be able to progress.

Other typical errors are to assume you can contribute as much as your partner and to discount the influence of the parent who has custody. There is no way in which you are immediately going to count as much in a young child's eyes as either of these two people. Later on, you might end up as the most significant friend or role model that the child has, but that is a long way off. Rushing confidently into a tight emotional twosome is usually regretted.

Nonetheless, optimistic new partners have a distinct edge over pessimists, whatever their original mistakes. The evidence shows that more of those who go confidently into the situation try to learn from the rebuffs they encounter: they change their tactics, they try again, and eventually they succeed. What they began with was commitment. They get more help from their partners (the child's natural parent) because this commitment is usually appreciated and respected. This in turn keeps their desire to help their ex-spouse and the child at a high level. A pessimist may be agreeably surprised—many are. But once discouraged, such a person has not much to fall back on, and little reason to continue. There is correspondingly less mutual encouragement between partners.

Of those who were interviewed who had not managed to continue a relationship with their partners' children in any meaningful way, most said they started with a premonition that they and the children just would not see eye to eye. This kind of prophecy fulfills itself.

Your partner and his children want to see each other, and it is good that they do so. Sometimes they fight and may declare that they never want to see each other again. But parents and children do that kind of thing. That is the more dramatic side. The good times include simply knowing that each other is still there, and caring enough to say hello. When contact is broken, it is not the end of the world, but it casts a shadow over both sides through the sense of loss, rejection, and guilt. The case studies in this book have convinced me that it is a mistake to sever contact. On the children's side there is confusion, self-doubt, nagging questions that are never fully answered by the parent they live with. The parent who loses contact is always wondering, too. He finds it hard to start afresh without knowing what has happened to his other children, and whether they need some help.

You can help your partner by not blocking the contact between him and his child, by encouraging him in difficult times, and by helping him get the most out of it. Your reward is a more complete person.

2 : Choosing a Role: Center Stage or Understudy?

Success in choosing a role means contributing to the happiness of each of the people involved, to the extent that they like getting together and feel that they share good times with each other. Different people have found different routes toward this kind of success. At one extreme, there are some who remain in the shadows, offering smiles, help when needed, but not much by way of conversation or ideas on what to do. At the other extreme, there are a few who have more or less taken over the mother's role in its entirety.

However, even those who have eventually become the key mother figure in the children's lives are likely to have started slowly and gradually. They have not presumed to move on stage, let alone center stage, until they have felt a loud, clear call in that direction from the others in the drama.

As mentioned in chapter 1, rushing into a "second mother" role from the first visit generally leads to failure, or at least to a long struggle. This kind of rushing is not thought of by the woman concerned as an attempt to supplant the real mother in the child's affections. More often than not it is far from being a conscious attempt to take over. But this does not prevent it from being seen in that light by the child, by the child's mother, and sometimes by the child's father.

Rushing is more often a well-meaning attempt to get everything onto a friendly basis as quickly as possible. It is natural to want to get over any awkwardness rapidly; and it is natural to fear that perhaps things are not going to be quite so cozy between the two adults once one of them brings their children onto the scene.

An example of rushing, as described by a very perceptive eleven-year-old:

> Suddenly there was this woman with Dad, who said "Hello, you two darlings, I've been longing to meet you." She bent down and grabbed both Jimmy and me at the same time. I *hated* her trying to kiss us. I just remember her face coming down on us with a lot of red hair. And she smelt funny. Perfume, I suppose. She was always getting on at us to do things. All that time [a weekend] she would come at us and ask questions. She tried picking up Jimmy [who was six years old], and he didn't like that. She didn't try it on me, thank goodness. We just clammed up and tried to keep out of her way. Dad told me off for being rude because I wouldn't say anything.

It is very useful to listen to how children describe this kind of encounter. They tend to see someone they don't know stooping over them and they feel trapped. They are nervous about the immediate familiarity involved in being picked up or kissed. The trapped feeling continues as they are aware that this someone is pursuing them. In this case, the impulsive lady with the red hair moved away not long after, and the boys got on much better with their father's next partner.

Fathers sometimes get alarmed or resentful when their new partner seems to come on strong with their children. They sense that they are going to have to split the visiting time between the children and the new partner. Instead of getting an hour of quiet play and conversation, they now find that this time is being used up by three people at once. There is still enjoyment, but it is of a different kind. The mutual understanding of what is being said and what is being left unsaid has been changed. As one father put it:

> I was very impressed with the way Stephanie got on the right wavelength with David [then eight years old] practically from day one. She has this talent for making kids laugh. As soon as

David decided she was a kind of licensed fun-maker she only had to put her head around a corner and roll her eyes for him to burst out laughing. They had a lot of fun together. I sometimes even felt left out of it. I'm a different personality, and so is David, really. I used to like the last half hour or so, just before I took him back to the car. About that time he used to unbend and start talking a bit more. Nothing very much—just anything that was on his mind, from what was supposed to be wrong with his cat's internals to what makes an engine go. This was the *ntural* bit—when both of us stopped worrying or feeling guilty and just got on with it. If I'm fair, I've got to say that Stephanie gave him a whole lot of laughs, and that was natural, too. But I was missing something.

Put very simply, this father was hit by three feelings at once: admiration, jealousy, and annoyance at missing out. This situation changed when David's mother remarried, followed by a compromise allowing two longer visits a year. The longer visits made it easier for everyone, particularly since Stephanie was pregnant and was not completely focused on contributing to the organization and the flow of David's time in her household.

Suspicion about what the new partner might be doing to their children are very common among custodial parents when they learn that the children are not just visiting their other parent, but somebody else as well. Where there has been a fight for custody of the children, fear of a renewed custody battle is only natural. Another occasion for suspicion is when the parent has heard bad reports from the child about the ex-spouse's *previous* partners. There is then no reason to believe that similar reports will not come up again—whether these have had to do with getting drunk, using drugs, getting violent, being fanatically religious, or whatever.

When suspicions well up inside the parent who has custody, they usually take expression in one of two ways: either the custodial parent will be concerned that the new partner will care little about the child's welfare, maybe even despising him, so that some harm will happen, or she will worry that the new partner will try to gain control of the child's affections by being a more indulgent, more fascinating, or more attractive "mother." This means, in effect, that anything from assuming no role at all to trying to steal the whole scene may provoke suspicion.

Please remember this: it is only too likely that you will *be perceived* to be competitive, even when you have no intention or desire to supplant the child's mother, but are simply determined to perform a limited role well. Your determination, in fact, just gets misinterpreted. This happens all the time. The more obvious your determination, the more likely it is that a suspicious person will decide that you are liable to steal the child's body and mind, and will set about making this as difficult for you as possible. Nor can you reasonably expect her to act otherwise. It is natural for her to patrol her borders fiercely and to protect what she feels is her own—even from an attack that is largely imaginary.

If you are "rushing," your role intentions will come under very close scrutiny. The child may be warned about you; he may have emotional pressure put on him not to get too close to you. In some cases an excuse may be found for terminating visits to his other parent altogether.

Businessmen nowadays tend to approve of "management by objectives." They feel it is good for them and for their companies to agree on well-defined goals for themselves and for those working under them. There are good reasons why this principle makes sense in a situation like yours, too. Of course, it is easier to go through life in a more carefree way, seeing what it has to offer and waiting to be surprised. But it is shortsighted to believe that everything will turn out for the best, with a minimum of planning, provided you just behave and react in a "natural" way. You should decide on a few of the basic things that you want to achieve in your relationship with your partner's children.

You probably have some short-term goals—like organizing the visits in such a way that no harm comes to the child, that all three of you have some fun, that the visits continue with your participation but that they do not interfere with a particular hobby or sport you may have. Short-term goals depend very much on your interests and priorities. There are many possibilities, but don't attempt to make an enormous list. Just decide, and then write down the aims that seem more important to you.

Longer-term goals are fewer in number, but they may also vary a great deal. You might decide, for example, that what you really want to help achieve is a situation where the child obviously feels comfortable about coming to stay, whether for short or long visits. Other goals may emerge from this one, like helping the child feel that he can ask any questions that he wants or that he has another home with another set of friends, or even trying to help him with any personal or behavioral problems he might have.

Limits on your involvement should be spelled out in your goals. At one extreme, you may decide that the child is getting totally inadequate mothering and support at home, and that somehow his acceptance of you as a "second mother" has got to be your long-term aim. In most cases this would be a mistaken view, especially because you would in effect be asking him to reject what has been the mainstay of his background, and you are expecting the transfer to take place when you only see him a small part of the time. But occasionally, where the rejection has already been made by the natural parent (whether consciously or as a gradual alienation process), your decision to aim at total involvement may be the best thing.

At the other extreme you may decide to remain very much in the background, to the point of avoiding too much direct contact with the child. You may decide this for any number of reasons: for example, not caring for the child very much, not being committed to a long-term relationship with your partner, or wanting to minimize emotional entanglements. You may choose a pattern of contact that is friendly but not demonstrative, putting the burden of emotional response fairly and squarely on your partner's shoulders.

Between these two extremes there are obviously a lot of degrees of involvement. The right one depends on you, the child, and the circumstances. But it also depends enormously on your partner. We are talking about *his* child and a situation that has come about because *he* is maintaining contact. If he is going to be pulling in a different direction from the one you've chosen, the prognosis has got to be bad.

Management by objectives works when all agree on the goals. At some point, and the earlier the better, you should talk over with your partner as fully as possible what you think is realistic and desirable for your future role with his child.

All too often people in your position decide to fly blind, without goals or role definitions, because this is easier than discussing the emotional issues. They find out a good deal later that both partners were pursuing different objectives. One may have had a secret fantasy that, as the child grew older, he would want to change his address and move in, while the other may have hoped that the visiting would peter out as soon as the child developed strong personal interests outside the home or as soon as his mother re-married. When this happens it is hardly surprising that the new partners are surprised at each other, disappointed perhaps, and that this has a confusing effect on the child.

When you talk to your partner, be open about any obstacles that you see. Often, openness is difficult. Here is a sample of those partner-to-partner comments that were hard to get out, that raised eyebrows at the time but made everything much clearer and easier from then on:

> "The basic trouble is, I believe he is spoiled rotten."
>
> "I'm prepared to like him, but I strongly doubt that he's prepared to like me."
>
> "You never actually cuddle the child. I believe he wants to be, needs to be cuddled. I'd as soon leave you to do that, but if you don't start soon I'm going to pick him up myself."
>
> "If I'm to be the person who stops him doing the things he shouldn't, I feel I should get some of the fun of planning the weekends, too."
>
> "If you want us to get closer to him you're going to have to ask for more frequent visits, and a couple of weeks at a time, too."

Those of you who have your own children will perhaps recognize the feelings behind this one: "How can you expect me to treat my own children one way, and yours another, when we're all together under the same roof?"

Even if you don't agree with the sentiments reflected in these comments, the point is to note that they are uncomfortable but sometimes necessary points to make. In no case did any of these comments cause a crisis. In each case they were steppingstones along the way to achieving agreement on goals.

All this is easier to discuss and to act upon if your partner already knows what role *he* is trying to fulfill. Most Saturday parents seem to know what they are after, whether their aims are realistic or not. To keep some level of contact going is often their main concern, particularly if there is a history of their access being threatened. But some parents living apart from their children are not at all sure what they want. Sometimes they experience a surge of feeling to get back on terms with their children, but then in the next moment they lose heart, or they wonder what it is they are really trying to do.

If your partner has not made up his mind, there seems little point in your trying to choose a definitive role for yourself. If he is uncertain about whether he is really contributing something to his child's life, about whether he is providing more confusion than enrichment, he cannot really help you define much yourself. Your best choice then is to accept an exploratory role, until his plans become clear.

There is plenty of evidence that maintaining contact with a child after separation or divorce is indeed helpful to the child, and eventually helpful to the absent parent, too. Part of your exploratory role could be to observe the child, and the child and the parent together, and interpret what you see. On the surface it may sometimes look simply like one small person pestering an older person for a new toy. But look a bit deeper. Aren't they trying to find a way toward each other? Aren't there particular moments when they seem almost there, making genuinely close contact? Isn't this worth helping out?

You may add to his life, and you may eventually have children with him yourself. But you will never actually replace a child from a previous marriage. Life doesn't work that way. Although your partner owes you the major portion of his time, and although your children must expect what a father normally provides, a portion of his time is owed to his other child. What is reasonable by way of this portion you have to work out together. But cutting it out, or cutting it down to a meaningless minimum, is not going to help him or you as the years go by. There is really no substitute for contact with a child who belongs to you yet lives apart. If your partner does not understand this, it may be up to you to tell him. There may be a need to convince your partner that it makes good sense for him to keep up contact with his child, and there may be a need to demonstrate that certain kinds of contact actually "work" without detriment to your relationship with him. This can develop into an unusual but a very worthwhile and realistic role.

Nonetheless, you must not preach sermons to your partner. He will neither appreciate them nor be convinced. Anybody who is preached at may seem to follow your argument, but is in fact looking for a flaw in what you say, something to prove you wrong. The best you can do is to comment objectively on what you see, making use of your exploratory role.

Gerald

Gerald today maintains a very good, friendly relationship with his two adult children, who are now in their twenties. Twelve years ago, he was seriously considering a move to South Africa. He discussed this idea with Mary, who had recently moved in to live with him. He describes their discussion like this:

> She looked at me very strangely and shook her head.
> "What's the matter?" I asked her.
> "It's not you, Gerald."
> "What isn't me?"
> "Just saying good-bye to your kids and never seeing them or asking about them again. I've only seen them twice, and I don't know much about them. But I think I know *you* . . ."
> "Mary, I've got to do this. The alimony I pay is crippling. Seeing them is going to mean cornflakes for supper for the next

five years. I don't want to bring you into that. I want a solid basis for our own family."

Mary looked at the ceiling and told me there was plenty I could do. I could declare bankruptcy. I could go back to school for a doctorate. I could decorate my boss with a Boston cream pie, get thrown out, draw unemployment benefits, and repair cars secretly at night. "In fact, the world is your oyster," she told me. "But the most important thing is not to worry about me."

I tried again. "You've seen those kids. They are twelve and ten. They don't need me any more."

Then she looked at me and came up with the coup de grace. "I agree," she said. " 'Those kids' *don't* need you. But from my seat in the stadium, Pete and Philippa *do*."

Gerald feels that Mary somehow read his thoughts and brought them to the surface. He hung in and kept on seeing the children. When a demand for an alimony increase was made, coupled with the threat of suspending his access, he simply said no. By this time, Pete and Philippa were going where they wanted to go. Every other weekend, they visited his home. Nobody stopped them.

Mary set herself a very limited role. But she can fairly claim to have had the maximum impact on the relationship by "winning the big one." She and Gerald have three children of their own. Part of the basis for their family, they agree, is the knowledge that a major responsibility from the past has been honored, not just swept under the carpet.

Mary kept out of the way during most of the visiting. She made the children welcome, occasionally did some baking, and intervened when a rock fight started between Pete and some children down the road. Over the years, Pete has liked her, but has never tried to get close. They keep on good terms, but have never sought out each other's company. This is no more and no less than Mary ever intended.

Not so Philippa. For unknown reasons, at age fifteen Philippa decided that there was only one person in the world whom she could talk to and be understood by—Mary. For Mary this meant a *total* role change, and at a time when she had a baby girl of her own. But she agreed to open the door and see what came through.

Late one night she got a call out of the blue from Philippa, who asked if she could take Mary's blue weekend bag to New York, where she was going to enroll in a modeling course. Correctly interpreting this as a roundabout request to talk, Mary suggested they visit a friend who happened to be a model. The same kind of thing went on for several years. When Philippa married, Mary wondered if they would stop meeting. But they simply met less often, and the conversations have changed character—less about joining eccentric religious groups, more about combining a career with having children.

"Very slowly I realized that I was becoming a cross between an older sister and a role model," said Mary, "without ever having had the slightest intention to be anything of the kind. If anyone had told me that I would be spending so much time with Philippa, or even that I would come to like her so much I would have questioned their sanity."

When a teenager senses that somebody is sympathetic and prepared to listen, he or she finds ways of getting through to that person. But anyone who tries too hard to gain a teenager's confidence is apt to get cold-shouldered. A teenager will be very likely to choose your role for you, regardless of your own intentions.

An important aspect of role choice is consistency: most children respect someone who continues as she starts. If you decide to start off by offering more than just another face at the table, it makes no sense to withdraw your overtures of friendship a few weeks later because you find life less complicated or less boring that way. If you sense that you have made a mistake in your choice of role, change gradually if you can. But do not behave like a chameleon. If you develop a history of vacillating between aloofness and bursts of enthusiasm, you make it very unlikely that there will be anything enduring in your relationship with your partner's child.

It is easy to confuse choosing a role with becoming a role model. When a child gets certain ideas from somebody about what is good or smart to do in life, he is fastening onto details that may or may not have been expressly pointed out to him. Sometimes a child's behavior seems much like his parent's—on a different scale, perhaps, but very similar—even down to his way of talking, his way of laughing, the look on his face when meeting a stranger, his attitudes toward the opposite sex. In these cases you can say that the child has internalized a greal deal of what his parent was offering by way of a model. But more than formal instruction is involved: a lot of traits and mannerisms are picked up entirely unconsciously, with neither party aware of something being transmitted from one to the other.

When asked to say who has influenced them—whether in terms of values, interests, mannerisms, ambitions, or dealing with other people—most teenagers will mention several different people, including relatives, close friends, acquaintances at school or work, or even a celebrity whom they don't know personally. We are an amalgam of our experience. And whether you like it or not, you also have the chance to become a role model. The specific role that you choose with regard to the child may not affect the issue very much. Whether you are going to hover in the background or take a prominent stance, the child may find points about you—from the way you talk to the way you dress to the way he thinks that you think—that he admires so much that he copies them, or detests so much that he deliberately goes in the opposite direction. Either way, you have virtually no control over this.

When somebody is "accused" of trying to be a role model, it usually means that the accuser wishes that he were able to be more of a role model himself, but cannot see how to achieve this. In the final analysis, however, a child will internalize or reject whatever he wants to. If somebody tries too hard to be a role model, by underlining the reason for each and every act and pointing out why other people are wrong in what they do, that person will usually fail. Nowadays, most children will at some point consider alternative life-styles, different ways of thinking and acting. Consequently, when they come across somebody laying down the law as if all this freedom of discussion did not exist, they will consider that person downright unrealistic.

Should you in fact "try to be a role model," you will almost certainly fail. However, you will not be able to avoid influencing the child to some degree or other, very possibly in some way that you do not at all suspect. The choice is entirely the child's.

The general lines recommended to you in choosing a role are these: lean toward a background role unless circumstances dictate otherwise. Above all, try not to come between the child and the parent he is visiting: they need time together, sometimes with you and sometimes without. Avoid putting any pressure on the child to get to know you or to understand you (except for his knowing what the rules of the house are and what is important from the point of view of safety). If he is interested in you, he will initiate conversation. If he is not interested, it does not matter anyway.

But what are the circumstances that might dictate otherwise a more active role for you? First and foremost, you may get a direct appeal from the child. Listen to the surface meaning, but be prepared for a deeper meaning, too. Mary had to change her thoughts about her role at Philippa's request, but she also felt obliged to talk to Gerald about it immediately. He had to know that his daughter was going through a trying time, and needed the ear not of her father, but of an older woman.

Then there is the let-down situation. Nothing ever goes perfectly forever. When there is a burst of open warfare between child and father, or at home between child and mother, you are very likely to hear about it. It happens sometimes that an older child will complain to you or, more likely, make it obvious to you that something is wrong and that he would like you to listen to him and possibly even take his side. Here are some problems brought straight to the person in your shoes:

> Ten-year-old Roger was very worried because his father resisted the idea of taking him back home an hour earlier one weekend. He could sense that his mother would be angry and was frustrated because his father's indifference seemed impenetrable.
> Nine-year-old Cathy and seven-year-old Peter were bored. There was not a great deal for them to do in their backyard,

and they had seen some other children in the playground down the street. But their father did not want to "lose them" during the weekend visit. They needed some freedom.

Twelve-year-old Robin was convinced that his future life and happiness depended on ice hockey. He was one of several boys selected from local teams to receive free hockey training after the season. But this depended on getting a ride to the hockey school. His mother was opposed to the sport and refused to take him. She urged his father not to buy him any more equipment. Since his father was often away on business and was disinclined to enter this particular fight anyway, Robin appealed to his wife.

Fifteen-year-old Marcia was not allowed by her mother to see a particular boyfriend any more. For various reasons, she considered it best to talk to her father's partner about this. What if her friend were to come over *here,* Marcia suggested.

This is simply a small collection of the appeals and requests that can arrive suddenly on your doorstep. You may encounter even more problematic situations, including child abuse, use of illegal drugs, and teenage pregnancy. You will have to use your own judgment on how to respond to any of these situations, whether you would encourage or discourage the child's approaching you for help. Here are several guidelines:

1. Try to decide whether there is a genuine grievance or merely a case of the child playing one adult off against another. If you allow yourself to be drawn in by the latter, two houses will reverberate with the sound of "But _____ says I can!" for a long time to come. Grievances, however, require action.

2. Ask yourself why *you* have been selected for this. Perhaps you are thought to be the one most likely to understand or the one who might consider the problem less emotionally, less as a test of loyalties. Or, you may be the very last resort. If any of these reasons seems to apply—as opposed to being picked on by chance—think twice before you refuse to listen. Links between generations are rare, and you may have something special to contribute here before the child withdraws his trust from adults.

3. Often the best advice you can give is, "I sympathize, but there's really nothing I can do. Talk to him about it again, and I'll help you from the sidelines. But you're going to have to make the first move. Would you like me to help work out what you're going to say?" You would not be justified, for example, in driving Robin to his hockey school in opposition to his mother's wishes. But if he feels desperate about this, you could help him to renew his battle.

4. When your advice to go back and talk to mother or father is not taken, only rarely should you break the child's trust and talk over what you have been told without the child's permission. (Rarely, rather than never, because sometimes a serious health risk may be involved.) If you rat on a child, he won't forget it.

You may be required to assume more than a background role from time to time. Sensibly, you usually restrict yourself to being helpful and friendly—protective, too, with younger children. But when there is a crisis you have to act first and foremost as a human being, not as somebody who has to consult a rule book.

Medical problems, for example, are cases in which you can only follow your conscience. Let's say that your partner's child is allowed by his mother to smoke. You may believe that he is slowly killing himself and needs to be stopped. If you have a nonsmoking rule in your home, enforce it. According to what you believe, that is the only thing you can do. One woman told me that shortly before the arrival of her partner's daughter she always put up an antismoking poster on the wall facing the front door: it featured an ugly, sick harridan with the last inch of a cigarette dangling from her lips and the headline "Smoking is very glamorous."

If you or your partner smokes cigarettes, and this is contrary to the child's mother's house rule, you must discuss with your partner what *your* policy is to be. If you take a hypocritical line with a child you will be despised for it before long. But encouraging a child to rebel against her parent in a way that that parent believes is bad for her health is not an easy decision to make. Try to get the issue out into the open—in the case of smoking, by persuading the child to admit that she smokes occasionally away from home. This makes it obvious that in the final analysis the child is going to be following her own wishes about what to do to her body. Open argument is preferable to breaking laws in a secretive way. The child may not relish this idea at first, but presenting it to her as a step toward independence often helps.

Similar decisions will have to be made over swearing, soft drugs, exposure to pornography or to violence on television or in the cinema, and sexual activity (your standards may be totally different, in one direction or the other, from those of the maternal home). The use of aspirin or other self-medication by the child can occasionally be a critical issue. But questions that involve morality pose the biggest problem for somebody who is not trying to make a child think differently from the mother. The predicament of the father's partner described below is not at all unusual.

> Julie came out to visit us for a month, when Roland and I were living together in Paris. She was sixteen, and very attractive. I don't think our telephone ever recovered from the calls she received. Now it was perfectly obvious to me that she was sleeping with the student in the apartment upstairs within ten days of her arrival. I talked to Roland, who was amazed. (He is as blind as a bat about such things.) Then I talked to Julie, and it wasn't easy starting because I'd never seen her before. I don't care what the hell you do or you don't do, I told her, but I'd like to know what precautions you're taking. It took a little while to realize that she knew nothing, absolutely *nothing*, about human physiology, contraception, venereal diseases, or anything. She just thought she was being sophisticated. To make a long story short, I put her on the pill, and I got her and her boyfriend to get a medical checkup. Years later Julie told me her mother had been furious when she found out, but it had never gotten back to me. Julie thanked me. Roland still feels I exaggerated the whole thing. But I've absolutely no doubt in my own mind that I did the right thing.

You may never be faced with this sort of situation yourself, and even if you are, you may not have to make a quick decision two thousand miles away from the child's mother. Your partner, hopefully, will be more involved and more helpful. What you decide may be quite different from the steps taken by Roland's partner— that depends entirely on your personal beliefs and priorities. Simply remember that it *could* happen to you, and that you may not be given all that much time to think about your answer.

3 : Greeting a Very Small Person

There are several ways in which your partner can help set the stage for your first meeting with his child.

1. He can help by not making it a complete surprise. For any child who is beginning to talk and converse, "We're going to be seeing Nancy today" is enough. Your partner's tone of voice should imply that this will be an enjoyable "extra," but neither a complete substitute for a normal visit nor a big production number. For tots, the father should offer one or two details for recognition. These should be simple and obvious, like "Nancy's got black hair" or "She wears glasses." A simple, identifiable detail helps a child feel some control over what is going on.

For children five and older it is worth saying—if it is true—that you will be doing what normally gets done during these visits, but that this time "Nancy will be joining in for a while." This means that the regularity of the contact and the fun is not under threat, but that the child may expect something extra.

Your partner may judge at what age to explain very simply, "This weekend I'd like you to meet Nancy. She's a very good friend of mine." For children eight and older, this is as good as any other form of announcement.

If Nancy has her own children, your partner could mention that aspect of the encounter, too.

2. He should make it his choice. Some children will demand "Why?" or "Do we have to?" It's best not to sidestep this by saying, "Well, she'd very much like to see you." This makes you seem more intrusive, possibly more worrying. A preferable answer is, "I'd like us to meet together. She and I get along very well. I'd like all three of us to have a good time." This way the initiative is coming from your partner. Any pressure is coming from him, not from outside of him. It helps if you appear as an invited guest.

3. He can make it clear that you mean something to him. Many children, regardless of age, may assume from too casual an introduction that you just happen to be a cousin of a friend who happens to be in town—or something of the sort. This may cause difficulties later, when the child has to readjust to someone who is obviously closer to his father than that. When the two of you meet, there should be no embarrassment if your partner gives you a hug and a kiss. This establishes that you are close far more easily than most verbal explanations.

Some older children may be curious about "Nancy" in advance of this, and will ask your partner questions. (One precocious eleven-year-old asked, "Is she your *numero uno* now, Dad?") There is no point in his ducking these questions, or in pretending that there is nothing special between you. Simple explanations are best: "We see a lot of each other now" or "We love each other."

4. He can give you some authority. It is important to agree in advance on at least a basic guideline for discipline. This is preferable to struggling out of a crisis when it occurs. If the meeting is in your home, he should explain that you "make the rules around here." In your joint home he should explain that you "both make the rules around here." No big speech is needed—just this basic statement.

It helps establish your position better if he consults you from time to time in a way that suggests equality and equal authority: for example, "What do you think—is the stereo too loud for the neighbors?" or, addressed to the child, "Please ask Nancy if it's okay."

If there is a sudden crisis, for example, if you have to dash to the drapes to stop his child from climbing up them, and if the child protests, he should support your action: "Nancy is right. Please don't do that again."

5. For an older child, suggest a point of contact. As children grow older, they will need to know more than that "Nancy has black hair." If they seem curious—and most over the age of about eleven will be—it makes sense for him to tell him something about what you do or have or are interested in. Up to the age of about eleven, personal possessions might be more intriguing: "She has a swimming pool at her apartment block" or "She has a Walkman you could try out."

As the children get older, they will learn more from a brief account of what you do and what you like doing: "She works with a word processing unit" or "She likes fast motorcycles." This may provoke a lot more questions and your partner might as well answer them if he can. But it does no harm if he says, "I'm not sure, you'd better ask her that." If he does not push this too hard, this will begin to involve the child with you before either of you realize it—this is really the easiest way to break the ice. But he must be sure not to build you up into a kind of superwoman.

6. He can avoid battles with his ex-wife about your meeting the children. It is entirely his choice whether the child meets you while they visit him. But it is a mistake, for example, to shout this across the front lawn when his ex-wife and children are on the porch. Few things are more guaranteed to give a child a bad feeling about meeting you than to hear the parents argue about you. It makes it even harder for the child to admit later on that he actually likes you.

If your partner avoids an open argument on this, he should still be firm. You are the person who is now sharing his life. It is then a matter of quietly telling his ex-wife what his decision is. If there is a fight about this, it will usually be because the ex-wife feels that a meeting will either disturb the child or give the child a bad moral lesson. Your partner must decide whether he agrees with his ex-wife and state his case accordingly—but he should avoid involving the child in the argument.

However, if he is genuinely nervous that such a meeting may disturb his child, he had best postpone it until he feels more confident: his nervousness will certainly communicate itself to the child and you will start the encounter with a strike against you.

7. He can correct some false impressions about you, if necessary.
When it becomes obvious that the child's mother has been "warning" the child about you, this will not contribute to a good first meeting. False accusations had better be dealt with squarely by your partner as soon as possible. One eleven-year-old boy on his way to meet his father's new partner for the first time, commented to his father in the car, "She's a hooker, isn't she." His father narrowly avoided driving into a tree, and muttered, "No. Not so." A more frequent piece of misinformation is "She took Daddy away from us." If the child suggests that this may have been put into his mind, it is best for your partner to say that this is not so: he may answer, "We both decided to get together." Still, there is no point in going beyond a simple denial. It does not help the child to be told that his mother is a liar, or anything like that.

Some false impressions are too subtle to be dealt with by contradiction. For example, one child said to her father, "I've been told she's very sloppy." This is an opinion rather than a fact. "Well, I certainly don't think so," is a fair response. A more positive suggestion would be "You have a good look at her and her home. You see what you think about that." Children will make up their own minds.

8. For a worried child, he can make it an incidental first meeting.
When it is obvious that for some reason his child feels totally opposed to meeting his new partner, there is little point in forcing the issue beyond the child's endurance. Whether it comes from

fear, aggressive feelings, or sheer jealousy of your time or love, it makes no sense to carry a child kicking and screaming into a first encounter with you. It will not do either of you any good. It is best for him to say to the child, "Maybe not today, but some time soon."

On another day, he can arrange a meeting on neutral territory. Halfway through the visit, perhaps in a hamburger restaurant, there you are. This needs to be handled *not* as a big surprise, nor as any kind of a big deal, but as a perfectly normal happening— simple introductions, casual conversation, keep the meeting brief. Subsequent meetings will seem much less threatening to the child once a simple, undramatic, and pleasant start has been made.

9. He can avoid exaggerating his children's virtues to you. This is between him and you. If he tells you how amazingly intelligent, polite, and friendly his children are, he is making it much more difficult for everyone. It is not good to exaggerate their faults, but the error is likely to be in the opposite direction.

New partners are generally more confident about meeting or- dinary kids than paragons. Some report afterward that it makes them feel more inadequate when the children actually turn out to be rather unfriendly or hard to communicate with. It can make a new partner feel that it is she who brings out the bad side in these angel-children. Others admit feeling slightly hostile toward a child who is supposedly so perfect: it is easy to see this, too, affecting a first meeting adversely.

Imagine yourself in a scenario in which your partner is shortly to arrive at your hourse with the child of his previous marriage— a *small* child, under school age. You have heard about this child, but this is the first time that you are going to meet each other.

On the positive side, you know that your partner is anxious that you should get on well. He is motivated to help.

But you have some misgivings, perhaps. Let's assume that you have no children of your own, and that the young visitor whom you are about to entertain is just three years old. What are kids like at three? You try to remember the various baby-sitting encounters you have had, and you ask your friends with young children for their advice. This is not the same, you realize, as direct experience. This chapter will not be a perfect substitute for that, but it will help to prepare you.

Do not think of a three-year-old as either an unthinking creature or as a junior adult. The mistake is to regard him as at one of these extremes. He is somewhere in between—and he is at a point in his life when he is developing at enormous speed physically, socially, intellectually, and emotionally. He has a long way to go before you could say that he works things out logically or is mature in the sense of having control over strong feelings. But he is learning all kinds of skills every day, and probably senses a lot more than you may give him credit for, even if he cannot easily put it into words, or discuss it with you. He gets tired quickly and suddenly, and one of the most useful pointers to watch out for are the signs that this is about to happen. Moreover, he is an individual, with particular likes and dislikes: you must not expect him to come out of a general mixing bowl called "three-year-olds."

If, like Nancy in the account that follows, you have not had much to do with young children, the day that a three-year-old bursts into your life can be both alarming and memorable.

Many first meetings with a partner's young child pass more easily than did Nancy's. But the happiest examples do not always make useful case histories, except as a reminder that there is a positive side waiting for you, too.

Nancy

"I was the younger of two children, and I didn't know a rattle from a diaper. Robert and I had been living together for about a month when he said I'd better meet his son sometime. He brought Gary around the following Saturday afternoon.

"I had some things prepared, more or less. I just guessed at the sort of stuff that might interest a young kid. I bought a chocolate cake, and had some popsicles ready in the fridge. I went around the bathroom carefully and put Robert's shaver and the aspirins away. I also picked up a jigsaw puzzle in case he got bored.

"Well . . . he was like a dynamo, racing all over the apartment, trying every cupboard door. When he found something that interested him, like a magazine or a carving of an elephant he would take it, put it on the floor, walk around it three times and go off looking for something else. I spent the first half hour following him around, trying to distract him, trying to slow him down. I put a crayon in his hand and actually guided it across the page of a magazine to give him the idea of using it.

"He got the idea, but the magazine wasn't enough. He ran into the kitchen with it and started drawing on the door of the fridge, the tiled floor, the counter top and one of the walls.

"Robert thought it was a great joke. 'Hey, you'd better stop doing that!' he said at one point. But he seemed happy just to let his kid run about creating havoc while I ran after him like an ineffectual sheep dog.

"There were several disasters that afternoon. The worst was when he ran behind a table to get away from me, tripped over an electric cord (pulling over a table lamp), and hit his head against the table leg. Floods of tears, then five minutes later he was off and running again. The jigsaw was a failure: it was far too old for him. Then there was that chocolate cake: I didn't realize he would ignore the plate and the fork and sit down on the carpet and just cram it in with both hands like a chimpanzee. That stuff went everywhere. Then he peed on the carpet. We had a confrontation, too. I didn't want him swinging on the fridge door. I asked him to leave it alone; he wouldn't. I said I'd get angry; he grinned. Then I started pulling him off the door, prying his fingers off the handle with one hand while tugging at his middle with the other. That's when the screaming started.

"The screaming just went on and on. It terrified me. I didn't know anybody could scream that long without turning purple. In the end Robert came and picked him up, calmed him down, and washed his face. And that was that. Gary had survived everything.

"But I hadn't. We'd been meaning to go out that evening after taking Gary back to his mom. But I collapsed. I needed a drink, a few cigarettes, aspirins and an early night. If I'd had to decide that evening, I don't think I'd ever have seen the kid again. And I was dead set against having any of my own."

That was five years ago. Nancy has seen a lot more of Gary since then, and has grown first to know him better, and then to like him. He has recently been introduced to her baby daughter. There have been ups and downs in his relationship with Nancy, but the long-term trend has been toward more frequent, more welcome, and more successful visits.

Nancy's first experience of being a proxy mom for the afternoon is by no means unusual. With her as with many others, there was a strong sense of awe afterwards at what Gary's own mother must put up with every day of her life. Knowing that his ex-wife lived alone she told Robert that she didn't know how she could stand it by herself. It increased her respect for the ex-wife considerably.

The first and most obvious question is this: Did the first meeting between Nancy and Gary have to take place in an apartment that the child did not know? This meant that Gary was being asked to get used to two strange things at once, an apartment and a person. At three years old you haven't much experience of adapting to either.

Typically a three-year-old does not make friends with another person, young or old, in the way that people imagine if they only know older children. They prefer playing in parallel with other children, and they are wary of older persons until they have a better feel for them, and an understanding of how they fit in. Gary might have got along with Nancy more easily at first if he had been able to observe her for a while, meeting her casually, before being put more or less under her charge and control.

That afternoon would have been better on neutral territory, preferably in a space that Gary already knew. Further, he should also have been primarily with his father, and only secondarily with Nancy, until they got to know each other better.

This leads naturally to the second point. There is no question that these encounters work best when *both* the father and his new partner are fully involved. There are hundreds of little signs that are recognized, often totally unconsciously, between father and son, by which they alert each other or reassure each other. When all three are doing something together, even a three-year-old reads a great deal into this. He perceives that Daddy feels things are all right, and so they probably are; that Daddy is affectionate with this new person, so that she may be quite safe.

From Nancy's report it appears that Robert's major contribution was to calm things down once a full-scale tantrum had set in. If he had been there earlier, and more often, he could have averted the tantrum. I would be the last person to criticize Robert for accepting the Saturday-parent job. But once accepted, it has to be done properly. This means offering his presence, his voice, his embraces, his smiles, and his body to be climbed over from time to time.

Gary's activity in the apartment comes across from Nancy's account as something like a visit from Attila the Hun. This is misreading the situation. He was a very worried little boy, and Nancy's well-meaning efforts fell a long way short of putting him at ease. Three is an age when a family breakup can be most disturbing. He was old enough to know who his father was, and to sense what he meant inside the home. He was not old enough to cope with the feelings of bewilderment and fright when his father left and did not come back. He was almost certainly hoping for a reunion between his parents, since this is what most children of that age feel as a compelling need. Gary was having to build a new kind of world, one in which he saw his father only at certain times and in new places, rather than a lot of the time at home. This is a long process, and an important one. A child in this situation may find it difficult to adjust to new people.

Nancy's first question should have been "What are *we* going to do together with Gary?" rather than "How am I going to entertain a three-year-old for the afternoon?" It may need coaxing, or even pushing and pulling, but if the first introduction is going to work, three people have got to be fully involved.

Nancy could have quizzed Robert about his son's needs, habits, preferences, and interests. He could probably have told her to forget about the fork for eating the cake; he could have recalled the desirability of setting him up at a table with a plastic place mat and a bib. He could have remembered (or found out from his ex-wife) what stage of toilet training had been reached. He could have helped choose a jigsaw appropriate for the age level. There are many more things that they could usefully have discussed together first.

Next on the list is the question of authority. Attempting, particularly as a stranger, to reason with a three-year-old is largely wasted breath. He is still a long way from thinking conceptually. The incident with the fridge door represents a problem of escalation. When a difference is allowed to escalate it acquires emotional meaning that goes far beyond what is actually involved. Soon it is no longer a matter of protecting the fridge door or of stopping Gary from hurting himself: Gary suddenly feels his whole person is being threatened, and hysterical screaming is his response.

Sudden use of force to protect a child from, say, diving into street traffic may be absolutely vital. You have to act quickly. But this was different. Had Nancy called out, "Robert, I'm worried about the fridge door"; had Robert come up and agreed, "Sure, he could hurt himself and the fridge, too"; and simultaneously had they said, "Gary, you don't do that here," while firmly lifting him off, then the result would have been much more positive. The important things here are that authority is seen by the child to be shared and exercised jointly, and that Nancy has definite behavior "limits" in her house that are recognized by Robert.

Safety has to be mentioned, too. Nancy was wise to think about the aspirin and Robert's shaver before the visit. (Far too few parents are careful about such things.) But the apartment was not totally "childproof." (The loose cord leading to the table lamp is a case in point.) Here again, Robert could have helped more. A checklist of household hazards and of items which are liable to be damaged by a toddler is worth devising before receiving a child into your home for the first time. You may decide that certain rooms will have to be out-of-bounds because it would be too difficult to guarantee the child's safety or the safety of your treasures.

One problem that occurs often but which Nancy managed to avoid is that of competition. This is when the new partner feels driven to prove that she is just as good as, or better than, either of the child's real parents when it comes to looking after a young child. A little of this is thoroughly desirable. But when a person feels guilty or liable to be criticized there can be a compulsion to overcompensate by trying to take the child over at every meeting, sometimes shouldering people out of the way to achieve this.

When the new partner is overcompetitive, there are generally three symptoms. Suggestions are made about the father not really knowing how to cope with his child, for example, "Here, let me fix the diaper. What do *you* know about diapers?" Other suggestions may point to failings (real or supposed) in the child's mother, for example, "I see we've got a runny nose to deal with again. Thank goodness we've got a warm cardigan to put on him when we go out." The implications are obvious. The third symptom is dominating the time and attention that the child gets during each visit, so that the interchanges between father and child and the sense of privacy and closeness between them become very limited.

The competitive urge can become a problem at any time, but in particular when the child is very young. From time to time ask yourself whether you might not be taking up too much of the time that should be shared by the child and his father. Leave them alone a little more if you suspect that this might be the case. Gradually, when the child is used to the three of you being together, this won't be a problem.

Until the age of about two-and-a-half (an approximate figure, since children vary a lot in their maturity, even when very young), a great deal depends on whether or not the child was very close to his father before the marriage breakup. Some fathers get very involved with their infant children while others do not. The more involved he was with his father, the more he was structuring his view of the world on that person, the bigger the jolt to his feelings when his parents split up and his father was suddenly no longer

Hazards to guard against	Objects to protect
Anything liable to be put in the mouth (infants especially will put *anything* in their mouths), for example:	Younger children Pets Plants
poisons, (medicines, cleaning fluid, etc.)	Anything within the grasp of the child standing on tip-toe: books, ornaments, etc.
food and drink beyond their stage of development	
cigarettes, matches, ashtray debris	Anything resting on an overhanging tablecloth
cutlery	
plants, flowers	If he is in the habit of throwing or kicking, *anything at all* in the same room as a throwable, kickable object
pins, nails, etc. (e.g., found in the carpet)	
Anything hot:	
hot plates	Anything that can be knocked over by pulling on a cord
stoves (top and sides)	
hot food or drink	Pianos and other musical instruments
steam	
hot tap water	
open fires	Stereo systems and records
Electrical or gas connections	Curtains, carpets, rugs, upholstery (danger from dirty hands, dirty shoes, urine, vomit)
Tools:	
garden: shears, etc.	
indoors: screw drivers, scissors, etc.	
Kitchen or laundry appliances (in use or not)	
Any room in which the child could lock himself, and then be unable to escape	
Stairs, inside and outside	

there. Conversely, the more variable or superficial the dealings between father and child, the less agonizing the break. The greater the anxiety that the child brings to bear on the meeting with you and the situation behind it, the more you are going to have to deal with mood changes that are inexplicable and with the child's nagging fear that however nicely the day has been set up, there is disappointment and pain lurking somewhere. You and your partner have then got a long-term reassurance job on your hands. If the child gradually accepts the new pattern for living, both of you will have achieved a great deal.

The chances of your having to adopt some kind of reassuring strategy increase markedly with every month that passes between two-and-a-half and five years old. (I am assuming, incidentally, that the family breakup is recent.) The older the child at the time his father left, the less likely it is that the two of them scarcely knew each other. A child of four or five, for example, who was three-and-a-half when his parents separated is likely to have been quite badly affected and to be only slowly coming to terms with it. He may be nervous about something similar happening again, and may well be cautious about getting too close to you for this reason.

Sometimes a child at this age will be actively trying to patch up the old marriage, and you may expect extra trouble if this is the case. Children have been known, for instance, to try to push their father's new partner out of the car at the end of a Saturday visit, and urge him to drive on quickly "so we can both go back home." There are many variations of this gesture. When this, or something like it, happens to you, try not to take it personally. Of course you will be hurt, or at least embarrassed, but remember that in his present state of mind the child would probably do the same to anybody. Defusing this kind of scene is hard, but if you treat it lightheartedly, like a practical joke that doesn't come off, you get over it much more quickly than if you discipline the child. It is *not you* who has failed when this happens. It is a reflection of how far there is to go before everything becomes calm.

In some cases (usually with children a little older than three) the child's mother has warned or frightened him about the woman he is going to see. One or two danger signals might be noticed by the father in advance, but unfortunately it is all too easy to disregard them. "No, I don't want to go back with you and meet Caroline" is not necessarily a danger signal. It can be simply a statement of preference. But if the child implores, "Do we *have* to see her?" and if he is tearful and distressed, this usually means a lot more. He cannot handle the idea of the meeting. He does not know exactly what it is that Caroline might be, or what she might do; unknown dangers seem all the more terrifying. Note that if the child cannot bring himself to mention her name (using "she" or "her"), he is more likely to be seriously worried.

Other bad signs are saying nothing, looking away, clinging to his father, turning pale, and going entirely stiff or entirely limp. (Any combination of these may happen.) Loss of bladder control that is normally functioning adequately can also be a sign. Being too nervous to accept food or toys from you may be evidence.

It does no good telling a frightened three-year-old that you're quite a nice person really. Words will mean very little. Marching up to lift him, hug him, and kiss him will only intensify his fear.

Say hello, smile, and keep your distance for a while if you suspect that you have been the subject of a dire warning. At first your partner should always be in the same room as yourself and the child. Only short encounters with you should be tried at first—preferably in the open air or in a space that he knows to be "Daddy's." Avoid too much contact, though you will obviously have to stop him from hurting himself when necessary. Changes of clothing are best handled by your partner. Your carefully prepared treats may be passed up, or tasted with obvious misgivings: remember that this is a period in life when fairy tales have a lot of reality for an imaginative child—apples may be believed to be poisoned by wicked queens. Like it or not, you have a share in the stepmother myth, despite the fact that the child may live with his natural mother for a long time to come.

Overcoming fear is usually easier when the child is not alone—

when his father is around, or with a brother or a sister beside him when the first introduction is made. Safety in numbers is a principle children instinctively understand. Gradually, when a child sees that the others are beginning to loosen up and enjoy themselves, this is a signal for him to relax. Separating siblings during the early days of your acquaintance is not a wise policy.

The more children you are meeting for the first time, the more you must rely on your partner helping you. You will notice very quickly that they compete for their father's attention, and that far from being on loving terms all the time, they shout and swear at each other, tell tales, and occasionally fight. They make up very quickly, knowing that they are committed to each other. Take their fighting calmly; it often boils down to a demonstration to their absent parent that everything is not right. When their father intervenes, soothes the ruffled feathers, and distracts them, they can be friendly again very quickly. You can best help the reconciliations by supporting your partner and helping quietly, not by jumping in as a stern referee.

A young child is aware of far more than you imagine. When there is simply a change in atmosphere—for example, when his mother is frightened or worried—a baby senses something. He may cry, go off his food, sleep fitfully, or have indigestion. If this is an infant's response to an atmospheric change in his own home, think what a toddler or a five-year-old may feel on foreign territory.

At any age, a child is aware of how people feel about him. Sarcasm, shouting, laughing at instead of laughing with, looks that radiate disapproval or boredom, are all registered as unpleasant or threatening. Even if he shows no obvious signs of comprehending what is going on or of complaining directly about it, he *feels* it. Sometimes people realize they can annoy a dog or a cat by swearing or laughing at it, but do not credit a young human being with a similar sensitivity.

Most children prefer to be smiled at, talked to, and treated as a person. A person is addressed directly, whereas a nonperson (like a chair or a plant) is referred to as an object that just happens to be present. If you are shocked by something or are nervous about the first time you meet him, this will show. But that is normal, and transient: you don't feel the same way for long. What can do damage is when you comment on him in his presence, assuming that he just doesn't notice.

Another crucial point is: don't rush. You may have an ideal sense of what constitutes mutual love between yourself and a child, particularly your partner's child. You may feel obligated to try to realize that ideal in this first meeting. Well, cool it. You cannot order love like french fries. If you limit your aim to that of making friends you risk far less misunderstanding and frustration on both sides.

4 : When a Schoolchild Crosses Your Threshold

hildren aged five through twelve differ from preschool children in a number of important respects. Depending, of course, on the development of the particular child, there is in the first place a greater likelihood that a period of regret or even "mourning" has been experienced after his parents split up. When the parents tell him that this is the reality of their lives, he accepts it. He doesn't want to, but he knows a bit more about the world and he is inclined to believe that acceptance is necessary. Moreover, he is likely to have had a more developed relationship with his father, and, therefore, the feeling of loss is greater.

If you are meeting your partner's five-year-old child shortly after his parents split up, you are meeting someone who has gone through a trauma and is likely to be grieving. His contact with his father at this time is extremely important to him: it tells him that he has not been abandoned because he was obnoxious as a child, and it maintains a link with someone who means a great deal in terms of a model to look up to and copy, someone whose approval is needed.

In this context, then, you will not be surprised to find a child who is bright and sunny one moment but distraught the next on account of something very minor. You might regard him as unusually sensitive, or perhaps as slow to mature emotionally. The fact is that there is a much larger problem with which he is slowly trying to come to terms. If you meet somebody at a party who has just lost his job and doesn't want anybody to know about it, some of the anxiety he is feeling is bound to come to the surface: you might notice that he, too, is behaving ultrasensitively and makes exaggerated responses now and then.

It may be hard right now for the five-year-old to accept any demonstrations of affection between his father and you, *or* between his father and your children, if you have any. The kissing, cuddling, nuzzling, and welcoming are reassuring gestures that he has just lost. He has assumed until recently that this was his exclusive right where his parents were concerned, with exceptions only being made for a brother or a sister. Consider for a moment how distressing it is to find yourself virtually supplanted by other people.

Without trying to put on a false front, you should make it seem as if there is always plenty of demonstrative affection flowing around. Four times out of five he will eventually want to join in a big hug with you and your partner. That is fine. Invite him into it, but never force him in. Nag your partner a little, if necessary, to make sure that he takes the lead in giving his child at least a fair share of holding, carrying, and the like.

If the child has been living with only one parent for some time, he may be less emotionally uncertain by the time that you meet him. He may, for example, have never had very much awareness of his father at home; his mother may have acquired an agreeable partner herself. Then again, this may not be the first time he has been taken to see a partner of his father. Any of these factors could make for an easier first meeting, since each presupposes a clearer sense of a pattern in his life.

You may find yourself perplexed by the superficial air of experience that some of these five-year-olds have. One five-year-old greeted his father's new partner with a casual, "Well, hi," then demanded of his father, "Say, what happened to Ellie, Dad?" A child who has learned to respond in this way is not really trying to be cool or rude: he is reacting as he has been taught by the circumstances around him. Beneath this brash exterior is a very ordinary young child who wants to love and to be loved by people he can rely on.

From about age five on you may find that the child has been recruited as a kind of messenger. When you suspect this is happening you have to be very careful to distinguish certain things, in particular, where the "message" ends and the "messenger" begins. A typical message episode goes like this:

> When Marty first came to stay over with us he had a dirty brown paper bag along with his overnight bag. As soon as I offered to carry both of these upstairs to his room he said, "No, *this* has got to go on your kitchen table," meaning the paper bag. Marty took it into the kitchen and emptied it. A pair of old sneakers appeared, along with a white sweater with dirty stains and a pair of badly frayed jeans. Marty then cleared his throat, and said, "Say, you guys. This is all I got to wear. When can my mom have more money?" All this in a singsong voice, like reciting a poem in school. It was such a pathetic attempt at extortion it was actually funny.

Not everyone reacts as good-humoredly as the woman who reported this story. It is harder to be objective when the message is directed right at *you*: for example, "Mom wants to tell you that we all pray to God every night that Dad's going to come back. Why won't you let him go?" There are various ways of dealing with this one, depending on your personality. The best and simplest is to give a sympathetic smile and say, "It's your dad's decision where he lives. But whether he lives at your house or with me, I know he loves *you* very much. He'll always want to keep on seeing you and doing things with you. I know, because he told me. Shall we go and find him and ask him about that?" This is not all that easy to say when a small pair of cold blue eyes is staring up at you. Reflect for a moment that this is not the child talking, but his mother. He shares some of her feelings, quite possibly, but he has not set up this scene. A more instinctual reaction—such as, "Get lost, kid"—may discharge your emotions and discourage repetition, but is not really fair to the child and makes it hard to reestablish friendly contact. (If you do let fly like this, make a brief apology when you feel better and consign that particular incident to the past.)

Messages are not always signaled in the convenient ways described above. As children grow older—you can be prepared for this from about their seventh year—they can become adept at transmitting messages in ways that make you unsure whether they are spontaneous or prompted.

> No sooner had he got into my car for the first time [this was his second visit] than Danny began saying how much better this was than his mother's old car. I hadn't even started the engine, and there was nothing so special about my three-year-old model anyway. Harry [the father] felt it might just be a spontaneous comment, but he hadn't heard him bad-mouth his mother's car before. I still don't know the real answer. It was near the beginning of a long, loud wrangle over alimony. I imagined this might be the psychological attack before the artillery opened fire.

This kind of uncertainty plays on the mind: you wonder just how far you can believe anything the child says, and you react defensively to what may be perfectly straightforward comments on what he is feeling.

Time and experience are really the only guides, but it helps sometimes to latch on to a comment like the one about mother's poor old car and exaggerate it to see what the reaction is. "Has the steering wheel come off yet?" buys you a little more time to think and gives you the chance to note any revealing reactions. A positive answer is a dead giveaway: "No, but it's very nearly coming off, I think" is demonstrating loyalty to his parent and trying hard to back up her cause in the best way he can.

A child who has been trained to give messages is often expected to bring them back, too. He may be pumped for information on his return, or he is given certain questions to slip in at convenient moments. The favorite topics are:

1. Money: Are you being 'kept,' or do you have a job? Do you have a good job, and are you earning a lot? Does his father still have his job, and is he doing well at it?

2. Personal possessions: How many cars? Who actually owns them? How new are they and of what make? Who owns the house or apartment? Are there any other houses? Are there any expensive habits?
3. Personal habits: What drinking goes on? Does anybody take any drugs? Are there other people in the household? What relationship do they have to yourself and to your partner?
4. Your personal history: Have you been married to anyone else? Do you have children? Are you more of a "homemaker," or a "career woman"?

Occasionally, too, the "messenger" may be required to report back on contacts made with relatives or friends. Where a traditional view of marriage breakup is held—according to which the relatives and friends have to choose sides—checking up can become a compulsive occupation.

Many children are curious on their own account, too. The child may simply want to know more about how his father is living nowadays and what is happening around him. Boys tend to be conditioned to ask more about cars, sports, electronic gadgets, and jobs. You may find that a daughter will comment on the household. She may ask, "How does Daddy get his shirts clean? Do you do them, or does he go to the laundry?" She is probably conforming to a classical role pattern rather than seeking information for her mother.

While people like to avoid having arguments and fights in front of children of any age, there should be more concern to avoid this when the children are between five and twelve. It is, I believe, a mistake never to express disagreement in front of children: this is unnatural and it generates bigger problems when irritation can no longer be contained. But there must be limits. Several women in the new-partner position say they draw back sometimes when they reflect that the child in front of them may have seen and heard this kind of thing too often already. Probably there were violent arguments prior to tbe marriage breakup; as one put it—"I've no wish to make the child sit through an action replay." Children with this kind of experience in their background can become particularly sensitive. If in doubt, still say you disagree, but cool it.

Around the age of nine (although this varies considerably) children start to notice rules of various kinds: they argue about them and give them considerable importance. In the schoolyard they sometimes seem to spend more time codifying the regulations for a new game than actually playing it. At about the same time they are apt to consider one parent in the right and the other in the wrong. It becomes harder for them to continue enjoying the company of both sides without some guilt feelings or a compulsion to reproach one of them and to act aggressively toward him. Who is "in the right" is generally a foregone conclusion. A child in this stage is liable to discern in his father "the guilty party," and this casts you in the role of accomplice. With a little prompting from his mother, he may go farther and perceive you as the archenemy, and his father as somebody who has been led astray.

If you are suddenly confronted for the first time by a nine- or ten-year-old who wears a look of profound disapproval even when demolishing a batch of your chocolate-chip cookies, you may well have there somebody who is constrained by his rules to act in this way. It is particularly irritating when a child in this frame of mind accepts and enjoys the food or the treats that you give him, but restricts his thanks to his father. It is not easy for him to acknowledge that you have your good side, too—particularly not at the first meeting.

Children need time before they can see the world and its inhabitants in shades of gray. It is wrong to try to *force* gratitude out of somebody who does not feel any: it suggests that he was right to mistrust you, even if you manage to wring a few thank-yous out of him. But it is also a mistake to let a child get into the habit of treating you like a convenient servant who never requires compliments. This is a bad preparation for life.

You and your partner should agree fairly quickly on a strategy for politeness, and on whatever other rules you regard as essential. But don't crack a whip at the first meeting. Keep it low-key and clear: for example, "More apple juice. Sure. But we all say 'please' here." Your partner can do his bit by saying quietly to his child, "_____ put in a tremendous amount of work to get this super picnic together. Would you like to go over and say something nice to her about it?" This needs a sense of timing to get the desired effect. But it can do a great deal for your morale.

Visits to the absent parent—though still very welcome—may stop being the focal point of each available weekend for school-age children. This is just a matter of having more friends and more interests. A child may suddenly protest at the way his free time is being organized. This is primarily his parent's problem, but it soon becomes yours, too.

A child who is starting to get bored will be less likely to react positively to you when you are introduced. A halfhearted smile and a limp handshake is followed by a sigh and "Okay, can I go outside now?" You are included in the boring scene, once it is perceived as such. In such a case, it is no good trying to demonstrate what a fascinating, energetic person you are. But you can help by trying to encourage certain tactics that will help make visiting seem interesting again:

> Support any suggestions for doing things *actively* (anything from judo to hiking to arts and crafts), as opposed to repeating *passive* things (shopping, television, etc.).

> Support any ideas for involving the child's friends in the visits.

> Work at fewer, longer visits, where you can plan something more interesting, like camping, taking a course together, or helping on a voluntary work project.

If it is a girl who is getting bored, you may be able to discern the kind of things that appeal to her, things she has never been able to develop as activities with her father. Of course, she may not fit into a traditional female role and might prefer taking your car to pieces to experimenting with makeup.

In the end there is really no substitute for the company of one's own peer group. Brothers' and sisters' company is not enough.

Are there any neighbors' children who might like to come around, any neighbors who might like to organize a joint expedition to a park, a game, or a rock concert? Are there any games of touch football at the local park? What is the age range of local theater groups, dance classes, swimming teams, conservationist groups? Explore what's going on around you.

Your partner will undoubtedly be somewhat jealous if the visits turn into social events. It defeats the purpose to overload the program to the extent that he never gets a quiet word with his child. But variety becomes more and more important during this period: it will, in fact, help him to observe how his child is growing up. He misses out on a lot of what the custodial parent sees of how the child is relating to the world outside the home. By expanding the world of the weekend visit he can get a broader view, as well as create a more stimulating environment for regular meetings.

You will find yourself being drawn into other problems. What restrictions should be imposed on normal, lively kids who are growing stronger every week, with more and more energy to burn? It is wonderful watching the eyes of a young person who receives a new bicycle, a pair of skates, a skateboard, or a pair of skis. But seeing them explore the equipment's potential can be agonizing. What use is a bicycle if you don't make it zoom downhill with both your hands off the bars? What are skates without hockey? What are skis without hot-dogging? Few children at this age can resist a dare. And, yes, children do still play "last across the railway tracks"—grim statistics prove it.

You cannot erect barriers around a young person's sense of adventure without stifling him. But you are still responsible for him—picking and choosing is hard, but important. Forbid swimming where there is no lifeguard, forbid climbing on anything that carries or adjoins electrical cable, and rule on out-of-bounds things like expressways and railway property. Nonetheless, a child has got to cycle fast sometimes, to climb a tree. and to test his nerve. Many decisions are close calls: consult your partner, when possible, on these. But when you have decided that something really is too dangerous, you must keep to your decision—even when the rest of the gang is doing it. If you give way easily on something, the implicit message is that you are liable to change your mind on a lot of things.

School and schoolwork are playing a bigger part in the child's life now. Schoolchildren need to get class assignments completed on time. They get involved in various events, too, like craft displays, sports, and fund raising. Every so often one or other of these things is going to cut across the child's visits to your home.

In the past it was only the custodial parent who was encouraged to have anything to do with the child's school life. Gradually, this has become much more open territory. Think for a moment of the teachers who have had to become more flexible about visits from both parents—whether together or separately—as society's attitudes have been changing. A child may want both his parents to watch him performing in something or receiving a prize. All around him are other children from split families, some of whom *do* manage to have both parents attending school functions. But do not expect an early invitation.

While schools are learning how to deal with two parents living apart, in most cases they are far from knowing how to deal with *you*. You present them with a particular problem, since your presence alongside of the child's mother is felt—rightly or wrongly—to be a source of tension. It takes only one or two incidents or complaints from custodial parents to convince a school to be very cool to new additions of the absent parent's family.

Getting involved in the child's school life should be attempted only when the child obviously wants this, and when your partner obviously wants it, too. If you want to tag along just out of curiosity, think again. Assuming you are invited, however, suggest to your partner that he test out the ground beforehand by mentioning to the other parent that you were both planning to come, at the child's request. There is no point whatever in giving her an unwelcome surprise. Should the child subsequently withdraw his request, you should accept this. Pressure has obviously been applied. The child does not deserve to be turned into a rope for a tug of war. A withdrawn invitation gives you a lot of information: whatever your relationship with the child, his mother is not yet prepared for it to be put on public view. It is not worth a fight. In due course, when the child gets older, he will inform both his parents precisely whom he would like to have around on any occasion, public or private. Until then, it is not fair to inflict this emotional burden on him.

If the child is with you the whole weekend, some time must be devoted to homework. It will be up to you, as well as to your partner, to encourage him to stick at it. You may also be required to remember what exactly Pythagoras said about right-angled triangles. A child who gets some sensible help (how to go about doing something, not what the answer is) will be grateful for it. Several unpromising starts between new partners and children in this age group have improved dramatically when it has come time to give help at the homework table.

Children are more observant about everyday aspects of life-style as they grow older. Gradually there is increased curiosity about the way people live, and why, for example, your chairs may be very different from those at home. Comments and criticisms can get very sharp ("Why do we have to sit on these terrible chairs?") because observation is growing at a faster pace than social manners or tact. Comments on the color of your kitchen, the state of your yard, the way the garbage is disposed of, or the choice of food and how it is cooked may fly thick and fast. Some of these are little acts of aggression against you and against the breakup of the family. But it is not necessarily so. He is starting to make his own judgments. This is part of becoming an individual with one's own opinions.

It does not help to try to stifle a child's criticism—you would be asking him to stop becoming an individual. Nor does it help if you overreact: this gives an alert child a good clue as to where you may be vulnerable. The more obviously you are irritated by a slur cast on, for example, your macaroni cheese, the more you are asking for a series of attacks on your cooking. Children recognize a good weapon when they see one.

The best way to deal with critical comments is to accept them good-naturedly, but also to show that you can give as well as take. Don't be afraid to ask what's so good about the macaroni cheese at home. It is easy to make that sound sarcastic and unpleasant: obviously, don't stoop to that. But children respect and, usually, like somebody with whom they can enjoy rough-and-tumble arguments with a hint of humor in the voice. Accept the fact that some children in this age group will wolf down yesterday's heated-up cabbage alongside chocolate eclairs. Others will remove with extreme care every shred of lettuce, every touch of mayonnaise, ham, and tomato slices from your magnificent sandwich creation: these they will leave in a pile and then they will gingerly munch the bread, carefully avoiding the crust! When confronting pickiness at the table some new partners become alarmed and guilty, thinking that this must be a reaction against them. Not so. From a large sample of new partners interviewed, there were reports of every different sort of attitude toward food, even when the children were at the height of their "loyalty to mother" phase.

How much or what a child eats is not very important. During a short visit, there is no point whatever in worrying about food. A longer visit, say, over a long weekend, requires more thought and planning. Remember this: drinking some liquid is crucial, whereas eating over a three-day period is desirable but less critical. Find out from your partner what foods the child likes and be sure to offer at least some of this. You cannot insure a balanced diet over the first weekend. The child may be suspicious of you and what you serve, and he may be too excited to be hungry. But you can make certain that there are several liquid alternatives available (juices, soft drinks, milk) of which at least one will go down the right way.

Breakfast is the most important meal of the day. Find out what breakfast cereal he prefers. If he likes a hot breakfast, make sure he knows that both his father and you have shared in preparing it. A suspicious child in a strange house will prefer one identical egg over another if he thinks his father cooked it. But show you joined in: you don't want him to remain at the point of insisting on Daddy's cooking. Note that in the short term it is much easier to give a child who is visiting you what *he* wants to eat and drink, within reason. No explanations will sway a child who has got used to certain things being "correct" from his life at home.

Wilma

Wilma, aged nine, was a very picky eater. The first day of a long weekend, she ate five cookies and drank some apple juice. Nothing else, despite pressure from her father and his new partner. Feeling thoroughly rejected, the new partner asked Wilma shortly before she fell asleep, "Is there anything you like to eat, Wilma?" She got a reply, and drove to a store. The next morning she saw Wilma smile at the breakfast table. There was the familiar box of cereal, and there was the bowl right next to it. Then, after a few spoonfuls, Wilma looked more and more doubtful. Finally she threw up. "You've ruined it!" she wailed. The problem was skim milk; only whole milk was used at home.

Three years later Wilma still had her preferences, but was perfectly prepared to try new foods. Understandably, however, it is that first long visit that has stuck in the new partner's mind.

It is too easy to make your relations with the child sound like an obstacle course with hazards at every turn. This would be a false picture. Children can be helpful and encouraging when you least expect it. They still feel that there is something important for them to be close to, despite whatever pressures and comments may come from home. You have a privileged position in being able to watch and help organize these encounters. When their moods change children may be perplexing, but they are always fascinating.

Since you are sharing these occasional glimpses of the child and his development, you will probably be drawn into one of the most intriguing detective games in the world. After a visit there is usually some kind of nagging question: "Did he really mean that, about liking/disliking school?" "Does she enjoy her music lessons, or is she just saying that for us?" "He reads very well, but how much does he understand of what he reads?" These are the sort of questions that all parents debate sometimes. But a Saturday parent and his new partner have fewer clues to work with. They are assembling a jigsaw puzzle without having seen the original picture. When the elements fall into place and you understand better what kind of a person the child is, with what aptitudes, interests, good and bad traits, there is much more satisfaction. In fact, you will probably never know—either of you—everything there is to know about this young person. But trying to help each other find out as much as you can brings a lot of pleasure.

A final point concerns physical contact. If you are meeting a school-age child for the first time, remember that at this age he sees his loyalties strictly in terms of black and white. Do not expect hugs and kisses. It is natural for children to avoid or to limit this if it suddenly seems disloyal. It is best not to meet this head-on: it may be necessary for him to reject you at first in order to come to terms with enjoying your company most of the time. Added to this, there may be, among boys, a feeling that it is unmanly to want hugs and kisses. If this is the way that a young masculine ego sees life, it doesn't help to force cuddling on him. In good time he will probably warm up, depending on how demonstrative his father is. And that goes for his sister, as well.

5 : Confronting a Teenager for the First Time

Many have found it particularly unnerving to be introduced to their partner's teenage child for the first time. This goes for both male and female teenagers. The new partner often feels that she is being scrutinized in a much more direct way than she had been expecting. She feels that her relationship with her partner is being examined at the same time. Often, the new partner is in for a jolt. Surely, she feels, those are not a child's eyes that are making their assessment with such a cool, knowing look? Why isn't it *me* who is doing the assessing?

Later, most new partners find that they have overestimated the maturity of the teenager. The pugnacious, questioning look is defensive in origin. What seemed at first to be a blasé or cynical attitude is found to be a cover-up for uncertain feelings about the world, a pretense of knowing all about new partnerships. There may be some real criticism in the way that a teenager looks at you, but this may be directed more against your partner—for the choice he has made, or for making a choice at all.

You may well find, too, that the teenager exhibits an air of indifference to what the father does with the rest of his life, and how this might affect relationships with his children. But the great majority of teens from split homes have lost neither the need nor the desire to maintain contact with their absent parent. They are now old enough to curl their lips, shrug their shoulders, and act casual in a more persuasive fashion. This has not changed their strong curiosity about a person who shares responsibility for their existence, and who has left them with some half-answered questions about themselves and their childhood memories.

If you show that you realize the bond between them is important you can help both of them. If your partner says something like, "Well, they make their own decisions now," you can guess that this, too, is a bit of a cover-up. He knows that time is running out, and that he might have been able to get closer to these older children had it not been for the circumstances of the marriage.

It is all too easy to react to a cynical sixteen-year-old with a curt "If you don't like it here the way it is, then beat it." You will only hurt his pride and cause him to withdraw. A lot of time is wasted. This is largely because your reaction was to treat the teenager just as if he was an adult. Eventually that is fine, and necessary. But as yet you are not dealing with a fully developed individual. (The crossover point is entirely an individual matter: some are more adult at sixteen than immature "adults" in their early twenties.) Until proved otherwise, assume that a teenager is not yet fully mature.

The main thing your partner's teenager is looking for is approval—this is especially important to a child who has a sense of having been left behind while the noncustodial parent went off in search of a better life. A teenager may never admit this need for approval, and he may vehemently deny it if pressed, but the simple communication that "You're doing all right, kid," even if it is just in one of life's minor departments, provides immense reassurance when it comes from the supplier of half of your genetic material. Obviously it isn't enough for this to be said solemnly once. It has to be reflected in quiet smiles, kind questions, concerned looks when there are disappointments, suggestions of help (even if they are refused), and spontaneous pleasure when there is a success to report. These are the kinds of reactions that people can express to each other when they meet regularly and unhurriedly.

The approval that the teenager is after needs to come from *you* as well as from your partner. This may seem very unlikely—particularly if you have been laughed at. But a teenager realizes more clearly than a younger child the fact that you and your partner are a duality. You work as a team, and a teenager will analyze how well you work. He may even try to drive a wedge between you— more often than not, however, this is simply a gesture, rather like testing the strength of a line by jumping up and grabbing on it for a moment. More importantly, the teenager knows that your opinion is something that matters to his father. He realizes that you discuss people and events. He wonders how you have talked to each other about *him.*

A typical teenager will be on the lookout for signs that show whether he is accepted as a part of normal adult conversation, or is relegated to the sidelines like a younger child. Until he shows that he is bored or out of his depth, it is always better to include a teenager in a serious conversation—even if his father has a tendency to exclude him. You are proving that you accept him.

There may be an attempt to elbow you out of an early three-way meeting. Regard this as a test of your character. Teenagers do the same to each other when they meet socially or at school. You are expected to keep coming forward. They respect that.

Don't retire into the corner for the sake of keeping things quiet. When you are repulsed, remember that this is your family time, too.

He used to sigh heavily whenever I got into the car with him and his father. Sometimes he cut right across what I was saying, as if I wasn't there. What he succeeded in doing after a while was to keep me at home, maybe seeing my own friends on the weekend. They asked me why I wasn't out with *them,* and there was nothing I could say. I realized rather late that I was there to cook and keep the place clean for him and his father, while they went out to a football game or a concert. In the end I told myself this was ridiculous, and I had a heavy scene with John [the partner]. I asked him if this was how his first marriage had broken down. I told him that either he and I were going to get away just by ourselves, without his son, for one weekend a month, or I'd walk out. Going away was important because I didn't want John dangling on the end of the telephone—and, well, spending money on me for a change was important, too.

So John and I started going away for trips together. His son got curious about them, and asked if he could come along, too. Once we felt we had got the balance right, we went away, all three of us, just for a few days. It worked pretty well. I guess I felt stronger about where I stood and what I would stand for by that time.

This woman warns that your partner's teenager may try to "push you into a little hole and keep you there," if you let him. This is by no means a universal situation, but it occurs often enough to be taken seriously.

Some competitiveness for your partner's time and attention is certainly to be expected. Girls as well as boys will try this. A girl may try to impress you with the amount of demonstrative affection she can exchange with her father. There is a distinct competitive side to this. In the example just shown, some attempt was being made by the teenage boy to be like his father. What he copies are the more obvious traits, like going off to a football game while the partner deals with the house. The hidden side of the partnership, the support they give each other during the rest of the week, is not copied because the boy cannot actually see it. (There may be no model for this in his mother's home, either.) Hence the tendency to treat his father's partner as a kind of second-class member of the family.

The main point is that if you do not join in the organizing of what goes on during visits at any early stage, you may well find yourself organized out of them.

Teenagers often talk a greal deal. Moreover, the projects they have in mind for themselves and their fathers often take a lot longer than those enjoyed by younger children. All this may increase the time you are conscious of giving up. On the other hand, they typically go through phases of enthusiasm for their father and his home, and what they can do with him. At other times they swing right around and concentrate almost exclusively on their friends. It would be unusual if your partner's teenager did not suddenly disappear for a while in order to throw all his energy into sports, cars, or music. You may then have to be supportive of your partner and assure him that his child will surely be back again.

In every home where adults and teenagers live together, disagreements over rules are bound to arise. When a teenager appears for the first time, gently point out that there are some things that are not acceptable. The teenager imagines that things will be more free-and-easy in the father's home—particularly if the mother has given the impression that he has done wrong or, at any rate, disobeyed *her* rules. If something happens that you don't like, get your partner's agreement and explain precisely what it is that you will not allow. Do it as from both of you, but do it quickly. Trying to regain control of your house some weeks down the road is far more difficult.

All this is simply a plea for realism. You have to plan positively to enrich your life with your partner. You have several points in your favor.

First, there is immense curiosity about you and your relationship. Teenagers often carry puberty like an albatross around their necks. It weighs heavily on them. Sometimes they think of little other than sexual development and its implications—how all these things might fit into a pattern that they themselves would enjoy. Well, here is a case history right in front of them that they can study and contemplate: your partnership represents an alternative pattern to the conventional marriage and family setup, which in itself is increasingly questioned by their friends, by the media, and even by older people. This makes them very curious indeed, and ready to study relations between you and your partner right down to the fine print. This is not just idle curiosity, but more like a search for clues about their own lives.

Then there is the fact that you are their father's choice. A younger child will sometimes act as if you happen to be there just by chance. But teenagers know that you sought each other out. Teenagers are all too well aware of this process. Knowing what is special or unusual about you tells them a lot about their own father. What makes you special in his eyes may be something that can help them in their relationship with him, and in their acceptance of his values. They have some respect for you—grudging respect maybe at first, but admiration that you exercised this particular appeal.

Certainly some teenagers strongly resent the family splitting up, especially if it is a recent event. They will perhaps hold this against you to some extent, depending on the facts and on what they have been told. But they are more realistic than younger children: they know plenty about divorce already through their friends, and they have probably met second partners before. They may have been aware of the tensions preceding the breakup. In some cases, they even applaud the breakup when it finally comes, because it is a relief from all that tension. These factors shift their perspective, so that they are not necessarily as critical of you, or of what you represent. Occasionally the older teenagers will welcome you wholeheartedly, as someone who is making their father happy and "caring for him properly." All this gives you a better chance of establishing a friendly tone and being able to reason with them.

You may well have some other advantages too, although these depend more on your individual circumstances. You may, for example, represent an age group that is between the teenager's own age and that of the parents. A teenager may find your ways of talking and thinking just that bit more accessible than those of his father. Rightly or wrongly he may well imagine that you and your age group have gone through experiences that are closer to his own.

You may find yourself becoming a reference point, a person with whom arguments about life have more meaning than when they are conducted with either of his parents. But it is a mistake to start playing "influence games," trying to see if you cannot persuade him to go your way, or a totally independent way. Driving a wedge between a teenager and his parents is not all that hard, but it is disloyal and indefensible, unless you become convinced that the child has reached a point where it is vital for him to make a complete break from his parents.

It is often very satisfying to be the one with whom a teenager feels confident to discuss things. This will be partly a function of age and partly a matter of your being a little removed from day-to-day parent-child tensions. You are relied on, then, to see both points of view in a less biased way. This can mean that the teenager's experience in your home will be considerably enriched.

Sometimes it will be through you that the teenager prefers to raise "difficult" issues with his father. Being younger may mean that you can introduce, for example, such subjects as changing schools in a way that is more reflective of a young person's concerns.

One new partner first met her three teenage "visitors" when they arrived for a three-week stay from a distant city. The eldest was cool at first. She seemed anxious to know where her room was, and the washroom, and the nearest taxistand for getting downtown, and not much more. Just eighteen, she seemed formidably self-possessed.

Her hostess says that she "kept the door open" by smiling (with no little admiration for her poise), by offering suggestions for things that she might like to do and see downtown, and—significantly—by taking her aside and asking her advice on how to handle her younger sister and brother. (A little discreet flattery of this kind can be very winning.)

> Within ten days we had discussed, analyzed, and proceeded to reorganize the basics of her wardrobe. I had persuaded her to try low-tar cigarettes instead of the brand she was used to smoking. I had introduced her to my gynecologist—and not a moment too soon. After three weeks I told her, "You are really a crazy kid: if you want to go to secretarial college, go ahead. But why not aim higher?" That one took more persuasion, and from other people, too, I must admit. She finished her M.B.A. recently; she's doing okay.

Furthermore, you may represent an alternative set of life-style values. This does not mean better or worse—simply alternative. Perhaps you set a higher priority on vacations than on home improvements, or vice versa, than the mother, or even than either parent. Teenagers are very curious about that. It becomes rather like visiting a different country and learning about the people who live in it: one is impressed just to know that there are other choices and other conventions.

You probably have something intriguing to offer, whether it is that you have a pilot's license or simply that you know a good diet. It will do you no harm whatever to parade your interests a little, and to see which of them seems to spark more curiosity. Don't make the mistake of underestimating your potential for having something that could fire their imagination and get them to want to know more about you. One respondent despaired of ever being thought to be any more than just her partner's sexual partner, until the first time his thirteen-year-old came to her house (when his father moved in).

> I had two cats. When they came in, I suggested we should feed them together. Then I remembered that there were some old bundles of comic books in the attic. We dug around and found them. Later, when he was driven home by his father, he said that I must be a pretty neat lady to have two cats and a collection of comics. He told him he could understand now why we had got together. We've all gotten along very well ever since.

Older teenagers tend to find more mature things to get enthused about:

> . . . When he knew that I'd been to the West Coast a lot, he asked me all about it because he was planning a trip out there himself and he wondered where he could get some work. I described the cities I knew, and I gave him some names of people he could write to or call up.

> . . . I mentioned it was time for me to be going to my dance class and she demanded to know what it was like, did I have a spare pair of tights, and could she come along because she'd always wanted to get into that kind of thing. This came as a surprise because up till then I'd felt she was treating me like the wallpaper.

It is not enough simply to have something or to do something; you need to be prepared to talk about it, and possibly even to argue in favor of it against some preliminary criticism.

Another advantage you might be able to acquire is to come to know the teenager better than he knows himself. This demands study and the ability to draw back a little from the picture presented by your partner, which is not likely to be wholly objective. First, remind yourself of the pressures that teenagers face today, then find out through observation how this particular teenager tries to cope. Understanding the teenager on these two levels makes it possible to be more receptive to him.

One key factor affecting most of the teenagers you are likely to meet, whether male or female, is that they have been subjected to accelerated responsibility. At the same time teenagers have typically been given little chance to develop ways of coping with this responsibility. This is the basic dilemma of the teenager in the 1980s—especially when there has been a split in the family.

The physical and social forces that have been pushing the teenager into accelerated responsibility are fairly obvious. The age of puberty is now lower in Western society than it has ever been. The expectation among teenagers that all of life's pleasures and most of the vices should be experienced while young is encouraged by the media. Yet there is still a great deal of pressure from other parts of society to refrain from activity for which a teenager is not yet supposed to be ready, *or* to restrict this activity to situations where some element of responsibility is involved (for example, having one partner instead of several, and using birth-control methods).

Between these forces the average teenager is required to compromise, often in a way that is unsatisfactory to everyone, himself included. Society offers few guidelines. The teenager is aroused, but told to cool it. In a contradictory world it is hardly surprising that teenagers often rebel, make their own rules, or refuse to have any rules, and regard anybody over the age of twenty-five as hopelessly transmogrified.

However, in some cases another kind of responsibility may be operative. Your partner's teenager may have been exposed to some of the backlash of the divorce—in some cases, of course, this process may still be going on. From one side or the other—occasionally from both—the teenager has probably been asked for support. This support may have been simply that of showing sympathy or understanding; just being there to listen is often an important supportive function. Some practical support may have been needed, too—for instance, taking over some of the harder maintenance jobs in the house, looking after a child who is younger, earning money for household extras, for education, or for vacations. Teenagers often give support in very capable and varied ways. On top of all of this, today's teenager faces the difficulty of his own vocational preparation in a world where employment opportunities are changing rapidly.

When too much is expected of a person too quickly, and particularly when much of what is expected is contradictory, a reaction is to be expected. Teenager crime and delinquency are not really surprising: what is perhaps surprising is that they are not more widespread.

There is an important point to consider here. When you are faced with a teenager whose aggression is only barely concealed, who shrugs when you ask a question or who gives the impression he has seen it all before, then you are looking at somebody who is a product of our times. It is not your partner, nor yourself, nor family problems per se that are uniquely responsible for what you see before you. Countless teenagers in "normal" families are the same. Do not let your partner feel that there is something basically wrong about the two of you that has made the teenager rebarbative and obnoxious. That line of thinking is simply a blind alley. What should be on your mind now is how to encourage a more friendly spirit, not how to undo the past.

To achieve this you have to give a little and to show there is an open door. Money and gifts are *not* the answer (see chapter 6 for a fuller analysis of this). The occasional small token can help a lot, however. Wherever possible, make this something that emphasizes you have noticed that the teenager likes something, or has a particular interest. For example, if he picks up a magazine and finds it interesting, get the next edition for him to keep the next time he comes over. If some flowers in the yard are admired, pick a few so that she can take them home. It is not the value of the gift that is important, so much as its symbolism. It demonstrates that you notice, you approve, and you aim to please in a way that is particular to the individual.

Time is something to give as well. Ask a few questions about interests. Whatever the reply, be prepared to follow up by asking for more information—even if the subject proves to be far outside your own territory. Do not leap in as an expert, either, if mention is made of an activity you happen to know very well. This provokes a nervous clamming up. Let your expertise become apparent very gradually, and never in a competitive way.

> It was very hard getting anything started with Michael. When he wasn't out with his father, he would just amble around the house, making wisecracks, watching television but getting bored with it. Then I found out he loved swimming. I felt, "At last! This is it!" and suggested we go down to my club. He actually smiled. In the car he told me how he hoped to join the school swimming team next summer. But when I asked him what his best time was over two hundred meters, free-style, he started getting more cautious. At the club, I said I wanted to do a quarter mile just to get flexible, and that then we might do a time trial. This freaked him out, apparently. He refused to get in the water alongside me, and complained it was cold. He went in eventually, but stopped swimming whenever he saw me looking in his direction. Michael was very macho, and he couldn't take it that I could swim competitively. Maybe it did him some good in the long term, and I feel I made a mistake. I just wanted something we could enjoy doing together.

Possibly you have yet another advantage—your own child. Teens are unpredictable where children their own age or a bit younger are concerned. But if you have small children, teens can be very friendly and protective toward them. A lot of teenage aggression disappears suddenly. Girls tend to be more interested in babies, but boys may be very taken with them, too. Teenagers are fast approaching the time when they may produce children themselves. They are curious to know more about the realities of this. Moreover, they will usually tend not to regard a very young child as a serious rival for affection—he belongs to a different generation.

At the very least, a child of your own provides a diversion and draws attention away from any awkwardness between you and the teenager. You cannot retreat behind a diaper all of the time, but if you can persuade the teenager to help you feed or play with the baby for a little while, there is a much more relaxed atmosphere—even if the baby decides to howl.

But whatever the age of your own child, beware of seeming to tie the teenager down to him. Teenagers like to pick and choose when they will acknowledge another child, let alone talk with him, or do something with him. The idea of being stuck with a younger child or being used as an unpaid baby-sitter has little appeal. If they get along together, fine. But make it clear that your partner's teenage child is a free agent, to consort with your children or to leave them alone.

Perhaps the essential differences between greeting a teenager and a younger child in these circumstances is that if you prove to be successful in it, you are letting the teenager right into your life. If you get on well together, you will talk a great deal, revealing much about yourselves. This alarms some people who are not used to it. Others claim that this forces a kind of reappraisal of where they themselves are going, which they might not have made otherwise.

> I was prepared for his daughter Billy, but she still took me by surprise. She was a very mature seventeen-year-old, in designer jeans. She shook my hand confidently and told me this was an ironic flip-flop arranged by fate. Normally, she would be introducing *her* new partner to her father for *his* approval. But here she was, having her father's girlfriend introduced to *her*. "Well," she told me with a gracious smile, "I certainly ap-

prove." This was rather breathtaking, but she continued to handle our meeting confidently, and without losing the initiative. Within a few hours she had me describing my school career, and why it was that I never took a master's degree. I kept asking myself who this person was who had invaded my private territory so deeply, but without getting me riled. She certainly had a most winning way.

What was more difficult was her brother Jeff. He was nearly sixteen, and obviously very interested in the shape of my body. He denied any interest in girls, but they were an obsession for him. It was embarrassing at first just sitting down in the same room. It took a while to realize that I was just part of a category that interested him. At first it seemed as if he was determined to work out a complete anatomical chart of what it was that his father now went to bed with. I shouldn't have taken it so personally.

Between the two of them, they shook up my world quite a lot.

You cannot keep teenagers in a convenient compartment for long. The more you are successful in making them welcome, the harder it will be to hold them at arm's length. When they look around at you and your partner in the middle of a hectic Saturday afternoon and demand, "Well, what's next?" admire the energy. Don't just deplore it, or you may be getting older than you think.

The following chart highlights the main points of advice supplied by new partners who have encountered their partner's teenage child—and survived. You can benefit from what they feel they got right, and learn from their mistakes. There is one overriding message: Never give up on a teenager, or for that matter, on a young adult. Press for the counseling that the real parents may be too proud to give, and keep your personal door open even after they have been busted for drugs, made pregnant, jailed, or picked up in hospital after an overdose. The chances of this are small, but, as one new partner said, "When their own parents decided there was nothing more to do for them—this was the one time, I believe, that I really did things right."

**Getting Acquainted With
Your Partner's Teenage Child**

Do:	Don't:

Encourage them to talk about themselves:
    ask what they like and dislike;
    ask what they think about
      current issues;
    ask about their enthusiasms
      for sports, hobbies, and
      people.
	Try to listen more than talk:
	    avoid telling them too much
	    about yourself until they ask;
	don't lay down the law about
	    what is "good taste" or
	    "the right opinion."

Show that you expect them to be individuals:
    in what they do or think;
    in the music they enjoy;
    in the clothes they like;
    in the persons they emulate;
    the food they prefer.
	Don't treat them as if they are examples of undifferentiated "teenagerness":
	    avoid saying "you" in the
	    sense of "you teenagers":
	    avoid making unflattering
	    comparisons between them
	    and other young people.

Explain any basic rules of the house in a tone that suggests they would probably conform anyway (including sharing the chores).	Don't tell them off in the same way in which you tell off younger children (avoid doing it at all in front of others).
Be demonstrative with your partner: show affection in your normal way, in front of them.	Avoid giving them hugs and kisses until you are sure they will accept it without embarrassment.
Be open to questions and prepared to discuss anything. (If you feel nervous discussing something, simply say so, and ask for them to think about it.)	Ask their permission before repeating (even to your partner) confidences they have shared with you.

Be welcoming to their friends:
    suggest that they visit;
    ask after them.
Ask about any time pressures they may have (homework, music practice, etc.).
	Don't ridicule their friends, even if they do so themselves.
	
	Don't suggest that their work is any less important than any other work or activity.

6 : The Santa Claus Syndrome

Perhaps the commonest stereotype of the father who leaves home is that of a man who tries to buy his way out of his trouble. He feels guilty, according to this portrait, and giving money and presents to his children is a way of saying "Please don't judge me too harshly—look at these splendid things I'm giving you." Alternatively, or in addition, he is pained by the indifference of his children. Sensing that he is a long way away from them, emotionally if not physically, he tries to bridge this gap. Here he is saying to himself, "Listen you guys, you must like money and presents. Everybody likes money and presents. Accept my money, enjoy my presents, and we'll soon get back on a good wavelength together."

There is some truth in this picture—otherwise the stereotype would not be so widely accepted. Absent parents do feel guilty. They also agonize, especially after long breaks in contact, over a sense that they and their children do not properly understand each other. Guilt prompts purchases, too, as any jewelry store manager will point out.

But it is a mistake to assume that all absent parents conform to this stereotype. In some cases, guilt is balanced by relief at getting away from a situation that was too hard on everybody. There are also a growing number of cases where it is clear that after a marriage breakup the fathers are seeing *more* of their children than they ever did before, and are doing so with more enthusiasm.

Likewise, presents are not always a sign of guilt: there is also the joy of seeing pleasure on a child's face, and the opportunity to play with a train set together.

Possibly the biggest complaint among new partners concerns money and presents that are said to be "lavished" on the children of the former marriage. (Another typical complaint is about the loss of time and the disruption of the schedule.)

This dissatisfaction can be the reason the new partnership breaks up. At the least, it is often an irritation and a source of recurring arguments.

Shona

Shona comments on the last days of her life with Peter:

> I liked his children, and we generally got on fine. But I didn't like the way they treated Peter and how they always used to nag at him for things. We had a hard time making the money go around after Peter's company was hit by the recession and the alimony still had to be paid. When he was put onto shorter weeks, my salary as a secretary kept us in our apartment, paid for the car, and had to stretch to cover some of the alimony, too. This made no difference to Peter. His kids were just into their teens and they wanted bikes, electronic games, and disco clothes; he gave them just about everything. There was nothing he could refuse. I used to argue with him a little, but he said he loved them very much and he was sure it would all work out. He broke the news to me one day that we—he and I—would have to cancel our plans to visit my sister on the West Coast. I'd been looking forward to it, since we couldn't afford a hotel vacation. And I knew that those kids had just had half their fares paid to Fort Lauderdale so they could go and see Mickey Mouse on their March break. I was furious. I told him he might as well go down there, too, and put on his Mickey Mouse suit.

Monica

Monica sighs and pretends to shiver when she describes Darryl's easygoing ways with money and presents for his children:

We can laugh about it, thank goodness. And he listens to me sometimes. He tries, I'll give him that. But whenever Nora, his nine-year-old daughter, looks up at him in a particular way, I know immediately that he's going to end up buying something. She's got his number, all right. Seven-year-old Bobby asks for more things, but doesn't get half of them. Just hasn't got the knack! I think that Darryl wants to give them a good time so much that he won't let anything get in the way of their being happy. Everything's got to be perfect, or close to it. So even when we tell ourselves that it's going to be a cheap weekend, we usually end up wondering where all the money went.

There are some important differences between these two accounts, quite apart from the fact that Shona is talking about the past and Monica is describing the present with no thoughts of breakup in her mind.

First, there is a matter of scale. Peter was under a compulsion to provide expensive presents that went considerably beyond what he could afford. Darryl, one feels, overspends sometimes but not by a great deal. He still seems to have his feet on the ground. The difference in the children's ages works to Darryl's advantage here, since younger children are usually satisfied (with some exceptions) by less expensive items, and by treats rather than possessions. But the main difference is in the minds of the two men. Peter could not stop himself from buying expensive items for his children. Darryl can listen to criticism from Monica.

Another difference is the effect on the new partners. Shona saw her hard-earned money going not just into alimony payments but into lavish purchases as well. She was no longer in control of her own money, and her resentment gradually increased until it dominated all other considerations. Monica does not work and has a three-year-old of her own to look after. There is never any suggestion in what she says that Darryl's generosity to his other children is threatening her or her child's standard of living.

Another critical difference is that of identification. Shona clearly felt that anything Peter gave was a transaction entirely separate from herself. (One wonders if they ever discussed what they might give the children as birthday presents.) Monica's stance is different. She is involved, and her report reflects joint activities: "*we* tell ourselves . . ." and "*we* usually end up wondering. . . ." She has noticed a lot about how the children ask for things, and what happens when they do. It is possible, as happens occasionally with new partners, that she is just as much at fault as Darryl is. She seems rather to enjoy their joint weakness. There is an undeniable sense of pride in her noting his determination (hers, too, by implication) to give the children "a good time."

To some extent, this is simply a matter of economics. When money is no problem, gifts and presents are very much less of a problem, too.

If you have reason to suspect that your partner is shifting away from a realistic attitude on this point, you have got some hard talking to do. This may be painful but it is vital.

Another related problem concerns comparisons. Three kinds of children could be involved: your partner's children by his former marriage, your own children by your former marriage, and the children that are born to yourself and your partner. When there is a feeling on either side, yours or your partner's, that one set of children is getting more than their fair share of money and presents, there is resentment. Favoritism is more often observed by others than admitted by the person who is guilty of it. Not unnaturally, new partners who have their own children (whether from a previous or the current relationship) tend to feel that these children suffer when their partners are too lavish with presents to the visiting children. Meanwhile, Saturday parents may admit to occasional lapses, but prefer to think of themselves as scrupulously fair and objective.

It is hard to make an unbiased assessment of these situations. Comparisons tend to be more emotional than rational. There are several reasons for this, the main one being that the children of the previous marriage are *older*. This means that they usually have a clearer idea of what they want for a birthday, they have better developed interests and talents that cry out for stimulation, and they express themselves better and more persuasively when they are trying to get something. A two-year-old may be perfectly happy with a relatively inexpensive item, like a jigsaw puzzle or a furry toy animal; a ten-year-old may have friends with home computers and would like one himself. The argument that each child may be made equally happy this way sounds unfair to the mother of the two-year-old, who knows the difference between ten dollars and two hundred dollars. When she argues for more money to be spent on her child, she is consciously or unconsciously in competition with the older children. When the competition gets hot, there is trouble.

It makes a lot of sense to have occasional discussions to plan expenditures for each and every child. This allows the competitive side of present-giving to come out into the open. If you have children of your own, this kind of discussion is needed to avoid long-term resentments.

It is usually a mistake to go out of one's way to get expensive presents for a younger child simply because an older one is getting them, too. Once or twice this came up in interviews. It was invariably regretted later, as when a new partner plunged her personal savings into a rocking horse for a child who had already decided he was into tricycles.

Money, as opposed to presents, brings problems as well. The principle of allowances going up as age increases is usually understood and accepted. But many new partners feel that the allowance should come from the custodial parent, particularly if alimony is being paid. But guilt may make father shell out a second allowance when his child comes over for a visit. These situations are often "contrived" by the children, or even by their mothers, according to several new partners. One new partner reported:

> There is always something that Norma desperately needs when she comes over. She always maintains that she hasn't a dime left from what her mother gives her by the time she reaches our house. The last time she came she announced it was her period and she needed money for tampons. That was the best one! You can't say no to that. But there's always something—

no tights to wear, tennis racket needs mending, always something.

The partner in this case felt that Norma's mother had gotten into the habit of relying on the father to provide for things in this way, and underspent on Norma's allowance accordingly. Norma's father contributed because he didn't want any trouble, and because he did not want to seem stingy to his daughter. Significantly enough, whenever the new partner tried to discuss her view of this with him, all he could do was wring his hands and say, "I know. I agree. But what can we do?"

A lot of the irritation in this situation can be eliminated if the truth of the matter is faced squarely: Norma is, in effect, getting a second allowance. So, make it official. Her father should be encouraged to tell both Norma and her mother that because Norma is chronically short of money for basic necessities, he is going to give her a fixed amount per month. This, it should be stressed, is the limit. Then he should stick to the amount stated. The more predictable the payment, the less either the father or the new partner will feel they are being imposed on.

This is small potatoes, however. The big money is what is negotiated for music lessons, private schools, summer camps, special courses designed to foster a particular talent or to strengthen academic skills, and ultimately for college.

When a child is handicapped and needs special equipment or training, or even a room in a specialized home, the expenses are usually agreed upon and paid without much argument. Such a child attracts more sympathy and there is often no disagreement about his state of need. It is with "normal" or "talented" children that the costs of education start arguments. Who is to say whether a child is gifted at something, or that he would develop better at a private school?

When one child is being sent to a private school to bring out the talent in him while another is simply left to the local public school, there is a sense of injustice. Within a nuclear family this can lead to long-term resentment on the part of the less privileged child, and feelings of elitism or guilt in the other. In the past, intelligent boys might get their college education paid while girls of equal intelligence had money spent on clothes and a wedding. Society is still coming to terms with the resentments caused by this kind of imbalance. But when it is a case of your partner's child getting the good breaks while your own child is not having any money paid to upgrade his education, the door to resentment is really wide open.

Obviously, there are going to be some differences in what is spent on children. An academically gifted child who wins a place at a college on merit and hard work deserves some help to get him to go there: it may be that he is the only member of his family with an aptitude for academic work. But his brothers and sisters need something tangible, too. If there is a fund for sending one child through college there ought to be another for whatever technical or vocational training programs might be needed by the others.

Similarly, if one child's aptitude for tennis is being rewarded by a session at an expensive tennis camp, there is every reason for finding something special for the other children, whether in the form of camps, trips, pets, courses, or whatever. If this is impractical financially, you should question whether it is right for only one child to be getting a benefit. Speak your mind, sooner rather than later. Too many new partners shrug their shoulders until their own children grow up and ask indignantly, "How come *he* always got something, while I never did?" This can be a harsh surprise.

You must carefully observe what goes on—*before* it becomes the cause of a major war. If something extra is being paid by your partner for his child's education, talk to him about that: Is your child going to be able to get the same kind of advantage? What if your child proves to need it *more*? If you are living together, or about to, remember that it is your money as well as his. The priorities have got to be open to discussion at any time, if you are to avoid feeling sour about it.

Some children move rapidly from dependence to independence.

They pass through college, or they go straight to a job, and they develop their own way of living away from the nest. Others are not like that at all. They use their parents' home as a kind of base camp from which they make expeditions from time to time. The great surge toward early independence in the sixties has gone into reverse in many places, mainly as a result of a harder economic climate.

The chances that your partner's child may be one of these base-camp dwellers have been increasing. This is fine, provided everybody enjoys each other's company and there are no arguments about contributions toward housekeeping or expenses. But it often becomes an infuriating financial issue. If your own father and mother would have called an older child living at home a freeloader, you are very likely to have similar ideas. But your partner may be pleased that his home is viewed as a good place to be. Secondly, he may suspect that if his child is incapable of leading his own life without support, the divorce may be partially to blame. Throwing the child out, therefore, seems doubly unfair.

If you believe that you have a troublesome situation in the making, you have an obligation to talk frankly about it with your partner before it becomes serious.

Sandra

Sandra remembers that her husband, James, used to be very gloomy about not seeing enough of his son Hugh during his early teens. But about the time that Hugh dropped out of high school he seemed to rediscover his father. They were so delighted with each other's company that there was never any question about Hugh having to pay anything toward living expenses, although he managed to get temporary jobs in stores and warehouses. Sandra had her own two young daughters to attend to, and was never able to spend much time with him. Anyway, the two men in the family enjoyed fishing and golf together.

Efforts were made to get Hugh through various courses. He studied accounting for a while, but found it too difficult. James paid for his training as a computer programmer, as a shipping broker, and even as a photographer. But nothing was ever quite Hugh's bag. He went to Europe once, intending to live in Germany with a cousin for a few years and "find his ancestral roots." But he was quickly back.

Hugh works for a while in a warehouse, spends his money on a motorbike or a Caribbean vacation, and comes back again. He has moved in with a girl or two, but they, Sandra comments wryly, "seem to know how to throw him out, whereas we don't."

One of her daughters could use his room now. When education plans for her children are discussed, there is always a doubt in James's mind as to whether Hugh will need more money, which puts a squeeze on what can be offered.

Hugh is nearly twenty-five, and is asking for a car of his own, since borrowing James's is inconvenient. James seems unable to make up his mind what to do. Sandra is on the point of declaring that either Hugh will leave, or she will leave with her daughters. But she knows James loves all three of his children, and they all love him.

Such a situation is an ongoing battle. There is no telling where or how it will end. Talking to James one is surprised by the fact that he seems to *know* that he is being abused by his son, and he is pessimistic about the future happiness of the family. Yet he refuses to take any definite action against Hugh.

This is perhaps the worst case of "guilty money" being paid for so long that the parent—and the new partner, too—lose total control of the situation.

As ways of keeping a reasonable limit on expenditures by older children who seem adept at digging for more and more, you and your partner may agree to:

1. explain to the young adult that once he is earning more than a certain amount, a regular percentage is to be paid for household expenses (laundry, cleaning, food, etc.);
2. establish a fixed date after which he is to stop living in the house (perhaps returning for visits only);
3. explain that it will be fine to meet for a vacation somewhere,

but that he is to pay the fare to get there (or contribute to expenses);
4. declare that money to start a business, to move into an apartment, or whatever, is a *loan*, and that one loan must be repaid before another can be considered.

The initiative in this situation may have to come from you. What you are doing is addressing a problem that applies to many families where the parents are emotionally unprepared to state categorically that their children must grow up. This may seem a long way away as you contemplate a young teenager. But this is the time when you should start talking.

An assumption has been made so far in this chapter that it is your partner who is more likely to be lavish with gifts and money. Sometimes it works the other way around. It may be you, the new partner, who is determined to be liked, and who is the first to yield to requests for a new treat, trip, or toy. There is nothing wrong with this, provided your partner is not sighing and shaking his head, and provided you are not relying on these tactics to buy popularity. It's a question of degree.

You must have some agreement with your partner about what constitutes cheerful flexibility in the family and what adds up to spoiling the child. Expensive items are not the only presents that spoil a child: a long series of giving way over little things is just as harmful, both to the child's expectations from you and from life, and to your relationship with your partner. Children do not make friends with doormats. If you demonstrate that a combination of whining and threats can get anything they want out of you, you are letting them walk all over you. An interesting person is one who obviously makes his own decisions, who has moments of generosity but is capable of arguing and refusing.

In most families there is give as well as take. A common response to "Can I have a new watch?" might be "Well, I haven't noticed you taking out the garbage lately," or alternatively, "Well, you've been very helpful around the house so show me the kind of watches you've been looking at." When a child volunteers something extra or helps out in a crisis, it's a pleasure to reward him on whatever scale one can. Similarly, when a child asks for something expensive out of the blue it is tempting to ask, "What are you going to do to get it?" But if you know that he has been saving for it and is working to help pay for it, then you are more sympathetic and may want to contribute to the fund.

However, the principle of rewarding good behavior is often under threat in a visiting situation when the child may be with you for just a few hours. You don't want to sacrifice too much visiting time to washing dishes together. Emotionally, too, it is difficult. Saturday parents are unwilling to risk letting their child feel he is being treated as a convenient source of labor, although asking him to help cut the grass or prepare part of the meal would be an easy request to make in a "normal" household. This encourages a child to think that he never actually has to *do* anything to get something: all that is needed is to turn up when asked and to keep out of trouble—the rest is just a matter of developing a pathetic look and a persuasive tongue. This is a bad frame of mind for anyone to grow up with, let alone for making someone pleasant to be with.

People who feel part of a team are less likely to impose on each other. If it becomes natural for them to help each other out, it is because they are deriving pleasure from that, as opposed to getting enjoyment out of using people for the presents they can supply. Good teamwork is its own reward. It has to start with you and your partner establishing it early on, and being a constant example of it. In this atmosphere people can get better at anticipating each other's needs, preferences, and difficulties. Requests for gifts, whether large items or simpler tokens ot affection, tend to decrease.

Sometimes a child nurses a suspicion that some failure or deficiency on his part helped precipitate the marital crisis. Children are often unwilling to think in these terms because it is painful. Where they are *not* encouraged to cooperate and to do things actively in the home, they receive no approval. Hence they may seek tokens, gifts that satisfy for a brief moment, but get nowhere near the root of the problem. In another home, where everyone is used to joining in, there is a good deal of approval to go around: the children's father and his new partner get the children involved and value their contribution.

You can get the knack of giving a child a present that you know he wanted but doing it in a way that makes it come as a surprise. The nature of a surprise is irregularity. But it is wonderful for a child to come to understand that father and his new partner sometimes go in for surprises to show how much they love him and to show their appreciation for his help as part of the team. It means that he is valued, far more than if each present that arrives has to be wrung out of unwilling givers by tantrums and emotional blackmail. Members of a successful team anticipate requests by doing nice things for each other every so often.

You have got to take the lead in a lot of this. Judging from the case histories, you are far more likely than your partner to see what kinds of pressure are being applied and how he is responding to his child's demands. But you have to agree on exactly what tactics you both are going to use if you think that the gift and money situations are getting out of hand. There is no point whatever in your becoming Mrs. Nasty if he is going to continue being Mr. Nice.

7 : Discipline

In some families, discipline is a dirty word. Nobody admits to wanting it, or to applying it: discipline is often regarded as a source of more problems than it solves. It is thought to restrict natural curiosity, exploration, and generosity, while discouraging creative thinking. It is believed to make a child more likely to be devious and vindictive, and less likely to act pleasantly toward younger children and animals.

At the other extreme, there are people who feel that lack of discipline is the cause of most of society's problems. They see control within the family as necessary for the children's development of respect for the rights of others. They believe that discipline is essential to character development, on the grounds that an undisciplined person is his own worst enemy, as well as other people's.

Most people's views are somewhere between these two poles. They feel that discipline is necessary sometimes, but that a constant awareness of restriction and the possibility of punishment is not particularly healthy for a child or for the rest of the family. They want to be relaxed and friendly with each other, but to have some kind of safety net, too. For this they feel that some rules have to be laid down. There have to be reminders; and sometimes there has to be enforcement.

In this middle ground, there is frequent doubt and questioning. What kinds of rules are necessary to avoid accidents? Are certain types of irritating behavior more likely to disappear quickly if they are ignored, rather than opposed directly with a ban? How far should you relax your own idea of what regulations are right for a child, when many others of the same age are allowed greater freedom? At what age does it make sense to start easing certain restrictions?

Decisions about discipline are not easy to make. Few people will pretend that they know all the answers. Children react to discipline of different kinds in different ways, each having a different level of maturity relative to his physical age. Some learn what might be wrong or harmful by explanation and example. Others make their own mistakes for themselves. Some take angry words in their stride, paying attention to the meaning behind them and the purpose for which they are spoken. Others regard them as an insult, as a challenge to do even worse next time. Consequently it is far better to try to understand a *particular* child than to apply a set of basic rules.

Find out what your partner feels about the subject, and think about where you stand yourself. Your views are likely to be different. The quicker you discover what each other's convictions are, the better. Don't be nervous about asking some direct questions such as: Have you ever actually hit Bobby? When? Why? Would you do so again? Is there anything he did here last week that worries you, that you're going to make him stop doing? How?

You may already feel that your partner is too relaxed where he ought to be more strict, or that on some issue he may be unduly harsh or anxious for control. Open up that specific subject, too, and ask what he really feels about it. And (in case he raises an eyebrow at you) yes, it *is* your business.

The sooner you start, the sooner you will find out what the potential conflicts are and discover the kinds of situation in which you may fundamentally disagree on discipline. Try to take the suddenness out of this discovery. Start thinking about where you are prepared to compromise.

You may be asking, "Why am I reading this?" You are not the child's mother. The child's father is presumably in charge during a visit. Do you have any need to be concerned about discipline, or should you just accept the behavior that you are given?

The first time that your partner's child tells you, "*You* can't tell me what to do!" the phrase will reverberate in your head for days.

In nine cases out of ten you will *have* to exercise some form of control over your partner's child. It is inescapable. So even if you simply see your role as that of supporting your partner's decisions, be sure that you will sometimes be the one who has to make a quick decision.

Depending on the child's age, you may be the person who has to decide on: whether to insist on eating up food; whether to forbid raids on cookie jars or eating junk food; whether to turn a blind eye to something you know your partner would not approve of; whether to allow smoking in the house—if so, when, where, and how much; whether to stop behavior that may damage the house or other property; whether to stop behavior that is distressing the neighbors or other children; whether to apply the same constraints to them as you apply to your own children. This list could be made longer without any difficulty. If your partner says, "Don't worry, that's most unlikely. And if it happens, I'll handle it," try once more: "Fine. But what if you're not here?"

When you talk about discipline with your partner, don't make the mistake of being vague or euphemistic. It is easy to agree that "we must take a firm line" on marijuana smoking. It's hard to agree on exactly what you will do about it. Confiscation? Loss of privileges? Discussion with the school? Search for the source, and discussion with other parents? Or will you shrug your shoulders and say, "Sure, they all experiment with pot in junior high"? It is your choice, but be on the same ground as your partner when you act.

Avoid euphemisms like "paddle," "smack," and "spank"—terms designed to make adults feel more comfortable. If you are really talking about slapping, hitting, striking, say what you mean. Be certain about what you are agreeing to, or arguing against.

Two- and three-year-olds, for example, are continually getting into situations where they have to be prevented from hurting themselves or damaging property. If you say to them while you are picking them up and taking them away from a hot oven door, "No, don't touch that, it's too hot," they are being helped to get a better idea of what heat is, of what things are liable to be hot. You are contributing to the child's experience of what is safe and what is dangerous and giving him concepts to work with. Moreover, children realize more often than you suspect when they are being picked up out of harm's way. You are therefore building a bridge of trust, however slow and gradual it may seem.

Then there are two other categories of behavior that you may choose to try to control. A child may eat less than you feel he should, or the "wrong" things and not the "right" things. This is not the same as behavior that involves direct danger. But you still believe that you are exercising discipline for the child's own good. The second category is mealtime behavior. This could involve a tendency to play with food, to throw it, to take it away from the table and spread it around the house, or to hinder other children from finishing their meal. You are attempting two things here— to make mealtimes easier for you to control and to clean up after, and to help the child become a more likable person.

It helps to analyze the purpose of discipline in this way. It forces you to realize what you are trying to do and to ask yourself whether a particular battle is worth fighting. For example, you may decide that for your own peace of mind, and for that of your partner, some basic routine is essential at mealtimes: you all sit down at a table, and getting up is only allowed when the child's meal is finished.

However, if a child who is on a short visit is suddenly off his food, there are several possible explanations. He may not feel well. He may not like what is on his plate. He may be feeling angry about something. He may be anxious to get back to playing with his toys. Do you really believe his health will suffer if he misses this meal? Or that he will become picky and spoiled? Do you really want to fight a battle over this one? During a longer stay you may have more legitimate cause to worry about how badly a child is eating. But confrontation on this issue rarely works well.

With younger children, eating habits can present you with some of the most difficult decisions. First, you have to decide whether you care about table manners. Second, you need to decide what your priorities are. Some new partners decide early on *not* to care.

Maureen

> I decided that there was no way that I was going to win if I tried to make the kids eat as we do, to be neat and tidy about it. I wasn't going to say to them, "Drink up your milk" or "Eat up your vegetables," either. I reckoned that if they hated milk and vegetables, and if they threw them around the room six days a week, it wouldn't make any difference what I said. And it didn't really matter if they ate nothing at all when they're in my house because they're certainly not going to starve.
>
> So I just left it to them. "Here you are, guys," I say. Sometimes they eat, sometimes they don't. I know they like wieners and spaghetti and ice cream, so usually they get something they like. But if they refuse it all one weekend, I couldn't care less.
>
> The same goes for spoons and forks. They know how they ought to eat. At five and six they *must* know. But they like playing around with their food, so they always eat in the kitchen. That way I just have to wipe the counter afterward.
>
> The only trouble is, when we go out for a meal. Mel [the father] looks at them and says, "How come they're the only kids here who eat like pigs?" And I say, "Come on! They're the best kids we have." I sometimes get embarrassed, too, when I think everybody's staring at us. But you can't teach table manners one day a week.

Many other new partners take a different view. They believe that they can and should do something to control what they feel is bad behavior at the table. This is expressed in the claim that "for *one* day at the very least, they're going to do it right."

There is no question that this second group—the table disciplinarians—have a harder struggle on their hands. They are rarely, if ever, wholly satisfied. There is always something that they grit their teeth about and are determined to improve.

Mary Beth is an example of somebody coming from a more controlled background who felt compelled to establish rules that would apply to small details as well as large:

Mary Beth

When I moved in with Harry I had to organize his apartment
to make it work. Harry pays enormous alimony so we've only
got a box. If you can't keep it neat and tidy you might as well
stop living. So I got the kitchen cleaned up and working, the
laundry system, everything. Harry was very pleased, although
he can live in *anything*.

Then his two children [aged six and four] started coming over
for a few hours on Saturday. You can imagine how I felt when
they started taking the place apart. God only knows what kind
of life they are allowed to lead at home. I can only see it as a
zoo. They treated the fridge like a free cafeteria. They used to
look inside and grab anything they fancied. If they tired of it,
they'd leave it on the floor. As for sitting down and having a
meal together—forget it! They couldn't sit still and eat normally
because they never learned how.

Well, I *taught* them how. I developed good arm muscles that
first year because at the first sign of trouble I'd reach out to
my right or to my left and grab hold of their shoulders. "No
you don't," I told them. "Sit right down again. Finish your
spinach." They fought and they whined and they pleaded with
their daddy and asked to get down because it was so "bo-o-
oring." But we stuck at it and they became human, at least
when they're with us.

Harry was good. He just grunted at them and said, "You do
as she says." Sometimes it got to him. When the little boy burst
into tears and said he'd be sick if he ate rice pudding, Harry
turned to me and asked, "Does he have to? This isn't the army,
is it?" But we had to get control or we'd have had an even
worse time. Harry knows that.

Mary Beth married Harry. The boys are now in their early teens,
and they stay with Harry for longer periods. They get on reasonably
well, but Mary Beth indicates that there is always apt to be discipline problems. She puts these down partly to the "unsettling
effect" of living part of the time with their mother, and partly to
a resentment that they feel toward her. There is an impression
that the adults and the children tolerate each other, rather than
share a strong affection.

Mary Beth's complaints are remarkably similar in intensity to those of Maureen. Neither is wholly satisfied, although each feels she has coped with the problems of early discipline in the right way. But while Maureen regrets getting people annoyed in restaurants, Mary Beth is aware of a constant battle for neatness in the home, and for "respect." In both cases, however, the fathers cooperated, even if they did not entirely agree with the new partner's attitude toward control. The important element was mutual support.

During every single interview of partners who had come together each with their own children from a previous marriage, each partner complained about the *other* partner (never themselves) applying different disciplinary standards to the two sets of children. This started early—going back to the amount of noise tolerated from babies. In one interview, a very perceptive comment was made:

> George just didn't hear the noise his own kids made. Or if he did, it sounded more like music. But as soon as either of my two children started hollering, that was different—that wasn't normal family background stuff, that was earsplitting. Same thing at mealtimes: if his kids left their food, they were sick or allergic or needed something different. But if *mine* didn't finish anything, it was, "You're not going to tell me you're going to waste that good beef!"

Many people are like George. Conscious, in many cases, of the strains put by divorce on their own children, they are apt to make more allowances for them. This is quite apart from a normal tendency to feel approval for what seems like a junior edition of oneself.

A new partnership with two sets of children throws together two different systems. It is crucial to work at understanding what the other system is if the two partners are going to feel comfortable. Physical contact in the course of enforcing a rule is best avoided. This applies to all parents, really, but it applies more to you, given your more precarious position. There are, of course, exceptional circumstances, like stopping a child from doing something dangerous. Then there is self-defense, too. But hitting, even if it is hitting back, or to get out of the way, is not particularly helpful. The educational value of hitting lies mainly in teaching a child that this is how a stronger person deals with a weaker one. You can see children in schoolyards putting this lesson into practice any day of the week.

Nobody likes the idea of their child being struck by someone else. It is rare that a parent will accept this from somebody like yourself.

Imagine for a moment that the telephone rings. Surprisingly, it is your partner's ex-wife on the line. (Your conversations with her are probably infrequent.) "I understand from Kent that you struck him yesterday," she thunders. Without waiting for your comment or explanation, she continues, "I cannot allow him into a house where he is going to be attacked. Tell my former husband not to expect him next weekend." Now what do you do?

Sometimes, if you have been having trouble with Kent, you may be anticipating something of the kind. But it may come as a bolt out of the blue. Note the neatness of the revenge being taken: it is *you* who are required to give your partner the bad news, and it is *you* who will be blamed by him as well as by her. When he attempts to get access rights restored, it may become a matter for lawyers. If she is very vindictive, the ex-wife will get her family doctor to sign a statement giving his opinion of how disturbed Kent has been; the conflict will be very unpleasant. Obviously, it makes sense for you to avoid even the remotest possibility of a situation of this kind. If someone must get physical, leave this exclusively to your partner.

Do not persuade yourself that anything happening within your home remains within its boundaries. Anything particularly strict or unusual that you do may be reported back. Some mothers will then say, "Well, I expect you deserved it. What did you do?" Others will get on the phone with you and demand to know what you meant by it. In one such instance, the following comment was made: "Is this really your idea of giving a child a happy weekend? Or is it the sort of power trip that you need?"

With some mothers you can explain what happened and why.

If you believe something has been exaggerated or fabricated, say so. You can suggest that your partner give his version of the event, too, in case that helps. What you are powerless against is the mother who resents the child's visits. Here is somebody who has been waiting for such an opportunity and uses it to stop visitation.

If you are falsely denounced as a cruel stepmother, you will not feel particularly happy about it. But a child who does this is usually young (under ten), with a record of creating fantasy games, some of which he actually believes in for a while. It is less likely, then, that he will be believed: the details that he folds into the story may be too fantastic. Furthermore, such a child is very likely to be rather fascinated by you and may want to come back of his own accord, even if he has already told the world that he suspects you of baking children in your oven.

Another very common complaint made by new partners about visiting children is that they do not, as a rule, offer to help with housework. Some new partners institute a system of rewards and punishments centered round the work that has to be done. For example, any child who has not volunteered for help in preparing the meal has to do the clearing up. There are several problems with this type of approach. The main one is that work around the house, or to help others in the house, gets identified with punishment. What it teaches is that the smarter you are, the less you have to do in the home. There is no pleasure, then, in helping other people—the smart people avoid that as much as they can.

Another approach is to impose the housework discipline on everybody in advance. For example, "Nobody leaves the kitchen until everything is cleared away." But the stress is still on the idea that helping is a kind of imposition, rather like taxation. Nobody enjoys paying taxes.

The best way of dealing with this situation is to try to keep housework outside the area of discipline altogether. When there is a very limited time in which essential things must be done, you simply have to allocate duties with no questions. But the main thing is to establish the right tone.

First you have to agree with your partner that you are a family in which work gets shared and where each helps the other whenever help is required—whatever the nature of the help. If the two of you have very rigid roles (if, for example, he is able to say, "I would never lift a finger in a kitchen, but then I'd never expect her to help me in the garage"), this mutuality may well be impossible for you. However, most people nowadays can probably make some kind of approximation to it.

You have to live out this mutuality if it is going to influence the children. If you both say, "I wonder if there's something we could do to help," you clearly assume that the child wants to be in on this, too. Remember that if his mother has not acquired another partner herself, the child may not have much experience of adults helping each other out in the home. This is something that he has to learn about in your home. The earlier this principle is understood, the easier it is to practice.

Sharing the work is one thing. Sharing the planning is another. A child may be very quickly bored if he is shown a pot full of boiling potatoes and told to mash them. If he has been involved in the preparation of the meal ("Would you like to plan the supper today with me? Let's look into the fridge and get some ideas."), the mashing of the potatoes fits pleasantly into the context of what he is helping to create.

Ideally, you will want to try to get every member of the family into the police force, so that there is nobody left to police. Discipline then becomes an unnecessary concept. The price you have to pay is letting the children have access to at least some of the planning function, and you may have to live with some strange menus: "Say, I think we should have spaghetti sandwiches tonight." Another trade-off that is sometimes harder to swallow is this: anyone who is part of a willing team has a right to make himself heard in quality control. If your partner's child may be criticized for leaving a deposit of congealed egg between the tines of a fork, you must accept the same criticism from him. In fact, you should probably thank him for being observant. But not every adult feels like that, especially after a long day.

Don't expect that if you have escaped disciplinary problems for a year or so, you will continue to avoid them forever. All kinds of influences over which you have very little control can affect your partner's child. As a child grows older, he may go through a period of questioning your authority over him. New partners may find a boy or a girl at this stage a kind of "Jekyll and Hyde." One moment they are relating to you very nicely. The next moment they will seize on some minor issue—for example, what clothing they are going to wear—and deliberately go against your wishes. This is confusing because it is out of character. You may put it down to an off day or decide that perhaps you spoke too sharply. But then the same thing happens a while later.

They may be at a stage where they find a lot of things difficult. Not least of all is knowing what kind of value to put on what *you* say as opposed to what their mother says. It is hard to approve of both of their families at this point without seeming disloyal. If you understand this, and are firm with them without overreacting to their little rebellions, you will find that they settle down to a more fixed pattern before long. If they do not, it could be a sign of a deeper disturbance that may warrant counseling.

You are probably in a better position than either of the child's parents to assess whether there might be a serious behavior problem. Being a little distance away and not having your pride involved to the same extent, you may be able to notice danger signals.

The irony of the situation is that you may be far more reluctant to suggest that something is wrong. For one thing, it may sound like a criticism of your partner, or of the effects of the marriage breakup. And then again, you cannot claim to have known the child for as long as his parents have. But you may need to make a tactful comment before it is too late to prevent a serious disciplinary crisis.

Sylvia
Sylvia was on friendly terms with her partner's son, Fred, who came and stayed with them over weekends when he felt like it. His father, Alan, approved of this and encouraged him to come over when he wanted. Fred made friends locally; gradually he saw

them more and more, and less of Alan and Sylvia. "Eventually," Sylvia said, "when he was seventeen he was using our place more or less as a hotel." But they didn't mind that.

Fred was a high school drop-out who was trying to make some progress in electronics, partly on his own and partly at night school. His room at the "hotel" was always filled with stereo equipment, some of it recognizable, some not. While he was there, Sylvia visited his room only rarely, but when he was away she did her best to clean it.

Gradually she noticed several things. Although Fred had little money, he was always bringing new electronic bits and pieces into his room. Some of these were large and impressive. "They lend these out at night school for us to work on," he once told her, when she admired a car radio he was carrying in.

Then sometimes during the evening somebody would call and pieces of equipment and money would change hands. "Made a buck or two on that one," Fred told Sylvia one evening, when he had to leave the dinner table to answer the door. Next there was the article in the local newspaper about a teenage gang breaking into cars and homes, selectively stealing stereo equipment.

"I had to talk to Alan about it, and tell him I was worried," Sylvia said. "But Alan simply wouldn't listen. He told me that Fred just wasn't like that, and the idea was so crazy he wanted to laugh."

It seemed less funny a month later, when the police arrived at their house with a search warrant, and took away enough items from Fred's room to stuff two patrol cars. "He was still a juvenile, luckily, so not much happened. But it was embarrassing and frightening. At first the police talked to us as if we had been trafficking in stolen goods ourselves. I felt guilty because in a way I'd been almost expecting it."

New partners have also been known to be the first to foretell drug busts, arrests for vandalism, shoplifting, unwanted pregnancy, truancy, and running away from home. Note that these are not things that happen necessarily to the children of divorce: they happen anywhere, in any family, at any time. But the new partner is often quicker to suspect something unfortunate. Jumping to conclusions is wrong: you may be misreading the signs. But you owe it to everybody to tell your partner what you suspect, while there is still time.

One point in Sylvia's account is worth underlining. Technically, she and Alan could have been charged with complicity simply by having harbored stolen goods in their home. Ignorance would have been a weak excuse before the law. Luckily, the authorities used discretion. You must realize that should your partner's child use your home for anything unlawful you might find yourself being charged as an accessory.

Disciplinary measures like curfews or depriving money are really only signs of parental displeasure. They cannot change the child's way of looking at life or assessing what is right and wrong. Nobody gains in maturity simply through having been disciplined.

You can no more mold a teenager's mind to conform to your rules than can either of his parents. But you can remain for him a contact with another value system after both his parents have given him up. Possibly your most significant contribution will prove to be keeping a door open between your way of life and the one he seems bent on choosing. It takes patience and time.

The older a child is, the more difficult it becomes to suggest and introduce him to new activities and new friends. Yet this remains a far more fruitful disciplinary measure than making him stop something, or taking something away, or insisting that he does not see certain friends again. Throughout childhood a child is irresistibly drawn to something that is forbidden. But if stimulating alternatives are suggested, he may be attracted to them. It is not impossible to attract a teenager to something less harmful than crime or young criminals, but it is a much tougher job than, say, introducing a twelve-year-old to a badminton club.

From eating habits to burglary—the scope of this chapter has deliberately encompassed the most serious kinds of behavior problems at one extreme and very minor considerations at the other. It is worth looking at this spectrum occasionally to see what kinds of values are the most important to stress. Children find it easier to accept at least some of the viewpoints of adults who are not nagging at them the whole time to conform to ideals of neatness that mean more to the homemaker's self-image than to the common good. According to one young woman who has "been there":

> There was always something rather ridiculous about going to my father's home after he remarried and having to relearn all the rules. Rachel had very strict ideas about how her two children should behave, and she was probably terrified that I would contaminate them. Tipping your cereal bowl at breakfast to get the last of the milk—I remember that was a big no-no for her. I was three years older than her older child, and she never let me forget it. "How can you *do* that?" she asked me. Hell, my mother wouldn't care if I lifted the bowl right up off the table and drank the milk. Every month or so, when I visited them, it was like having to learn a new set of tricks. I think she wanted to be friendly, and she liked me coming and seeing my dad. But I could never feel like talking to her—you can't get close to someone who's always worried about whether your elbows are on the table.

This teenager, as far as anyone knows, has never been in need of special help or advice: the point of her remarks is, though, that *had* she needed help from this particular source, she could not have taken it seriously.

Those new partners who have gotten close to teenagers have all tended to do things actively with them. They do not try out ideas in a vacuum. They do not ask, "Have you ever thought of meditation?" They do say, "I've got a great idea. We're going to meditate. I mean, tonight! Come on, I need some moral support. I'll pay for your first class. If you like it, you can pay for the rest. I don't want to twist your arm, but we're going there *now*, and they say the people there are sensational." Other things to do with teenagers include voluntary work, renovating houses, caring for animals, helping other children, and starting up a part-time business. The essential ingredient in these ventures seems to be collaboration. They are things that you do together—at least during the early stages. Yes, it demands a lot of time; and yes, one of the child's parents would perhaps be more appropriate for undertaking it. But it is very rewarding.

If there are any general rules that can be given about discipline, they mainly concern children's reactions to it. The point about nagging away about minor issues until you effectively sever communication about the big picture has already been made. In addition:

1. Children appreciate knowing where they stand. If you are consistent in what you require by way of behavior, they will have some respect for your requirements. If you keep changing the rules, they will start resenting you, and your system.
2. The farther away your rules are from those of the house in which they spend most of their time, the less they will tolerate them. (Remember that you are setting up *expectations* for them, rather than rules.)
3. If there is any deviation between you and your partner in the rules you want followed, or the way you enforce them, the children will instinctively find it. Discuss; agree.
4. As in any other house, children will have no respect, and a good deal of scorn, for hypocrisy. For example, if a child is forbidden to use a word that father frequently uses, the child feels contempt for the rule and for anyone who enforces it.
5. Children appreciate being given a reason for any rule whose purpose is not obvious. This applies particularly to children whose parents live in separate homes. The more that the differences between the two rule systems seem arbitrary, the more confused a child becomes. Explaining things always take a little longer, but children's questions about rules should be welcomed, not resented. Questions like "But why am I not allowed to d that *here*?" should never be simply dismissed. When a child puts this question to you, he is in fact telling you quite a lot about himself, his background, and his state of mind. If your rule is worth anything, it is worth explaining.

NEW PARTNERS' ADVICE
TO EACH OTHER ON DISCIPLINE

The following comments are taken directly from interviews, with very little editing. They represent points of view about which the speakers felt very strongly, and which they wanted to pass on to others in their situation.

"If you get cross and bawl at them when your nerves just can't take any more, don't think it's the end of the world. Even if you don't see them often, it can happen. It's happened to me. I hated myself for it. I imagined this six-year-old telling his mom he never wanted to go and see Daddy again, because of that awful woman. But then the kid comes to me later and asks me if I'm feeling better. I hugged him like crazy. . . . It's not the end of the world, but don't make a habit of it."

"Don't expect a child to do things you don't ask him to do. If he never washes his hands before a meal at home, how can he possibly know that you're going to want him to? I was driven frantic by doors being left open, coats being left on the floor, shouting at other kids through the windows. I wondered if he was just getting at me. But my husband explained I was being unfair. I was assuming that at ten years old he would know, and of course he didn't know. When I talked with him long enough to explain how we did things, he was fine."

"Don't let your own child get too involved in disciplining your partner's child. My daughter Alma loves children, and being ten years older than Kerry, she felt she should take charge. Now, it was all right if I got annoyed with Kerry for tossing her cereal on the floor, but if Alma reacted the same way, my husband hit the roof. We had some difficult moments, with me trying to calm them both down, and them both telling each other how unreasonable they were. We worked out compromises of sorts, but it soured Alma for a year or two, and there were a lot of tears. I think I should have warned my daughter at the start not to get angry with Kerry, and to report any problems to me or to Donald. . . . He *was* unreasonable, I think. He just didn't want to think of my daughter having any control over *his* daughter."

"If I've learned anything from comparing Bob's kids with my own it's that some kids will act responsibly with just the occasional nudge in the right direction, while others are constantly thinking up new ways of making your hair turn white. You need the same rules for each child. But you also need a smile for one and a baseball bat for the other. Some children are quiet and others are wild. Nothing you can do will stop that. The wild ones will only pay attention when you raise your voice. And you've got to push their father into it, too—to raise his voice with yours."

"When your lover's child comes into your home for the first time, he's on foreign territory, at least to start with. I think I must have been guilty of the two worst things possible. I realize that now, but I didn't at the time. I told him if he touched anything in my apartment his dad would be really mad at him. And when he made a mess, I took his teddy bear and his blanket out of the room and pretended to throw them out of the window. Well, for a young kid on foreign soil, that really was too much. I wouldn't dream of doing that now. I knew so little about kids! He was scared of me, you know? He used to scream when the car stopped at the apartment block."

"People are too afraid to argue with teenagers. I love arguing with them—especially my husband's kids. I win some and lose some; it's a challenge. I think I get through to them sometimes. My husband wouldn't dare. He's afraid of arguing with them at all seriously, in case they win. But I like it. His kids like to think they have no inhibitions—you know, they talk about blow jobs and stuff—but they're amazingly underinformed. They don't accept all I say; nobody does at seventeen, unless he's a real fool. But I like to think I've made some impact. They still get drunk at football games, but now they won't drive if they've been drinking. That's not just me, but we did talk about it. And now they know what herpes is, and how you get it. Don't ask me if that's changed anything, but I imagine it has. They're not perfect—but we have great arguments!"

"Don't offer rewards for good behavior. It's like building yourself your very own treadmill. Once a child realizes you're prepared to pay him for not doing something you hate, that's the end. It makes him figure out the best ways of getting you to offer more and more and more. He'll remind you every so often just what it was that you disliked so much, to make you up the payments. Say he does something like playing with all the controls on the stereo. Tell him to stop. Just that. Make him stop. Whatever. Only don't offer him ice cream if he agrees to stop. That way lies madness."

8 : Communication

There are three kinds of necessary communication that you may find difficult. The first of these is basic communication with your partner's child. The second is between you and your partner's ex-wife. The third, which will be discussed at the end of this chapter, may be the least problematic or it may be peculiarly painful—this is communication between yourself and your partner concerning his child. Each of these lines of contact has its own patterns of difficulty that you must be prepared to recognize.

Some people find talking to children the most natural thing in the world. Others, the majority, have to develop the skill.

What can be tricky is changing the mood and pace of a conversation without misunderstanding or embarrassment. Children who are adjusting to a divorce situation are learning to accept you in one kind of role or relationship, but need time and experience to fit you into another. For example, they may be enjoying a lighthearted, joking sort of discussion with you and your partner in a situation like a family picnic. Then you suddenly have to get serious. When you stop being a pleasant acquaintance in a playground and take on the authority of someone who is in charge, the change is confusing. This confusion for the child may arise when you suddenly ask such questions as:

"Do you need a diaper change?"

"What's that blood on your hand? Have you cut yourself? Let me see . . ."

"Isn't there some homework you should be doing?"

"What does your mother like you to wear outside now that it's colder?"

and so forth. It's important to get a clear answer. But, inexplicably, the child stubbornly mishears you, avoids you, laughs, or changes the subject.

You have a dilemma. On the one hand, you do not want to hurt the child's feelings or damage communication by pushing too hard. On the other hand, there are obvious practical considerations.

"Would you like to tell your Daddy, then?" is a useful response. It gives the child an escape route back to a relationship with which he feels more secure. No pride is hurt. But you cannot appeal to your partner all the time to accomplish a change of mood and get an answer.

Patience helps. If you are cross, if you say sternly, "Listen to me," picking the child up by the shoulders and shaking him, you give him a very good reason to lose confidence in you. Yet you cannot wait forever for an answer. You should take him by the hand gently and say, "OK, I think I've got the message," and lead him to the bathroom, or wherever. You are supplying a reply for him, and making it easier for him to adapt to your change of mood and role. You are showing that you are a quiet but determined person, who intends to get things organized in a practical way. If your interpretation is in fact wrong—for example, if the blood on his hand turns out to be tomato juice—he can always tell you. You can make a joke about it. At the same time he now knows that you are concerned about him, and that occasionally you will be acting in a concerned way.

When a child is shy, embarrassed, or aggressive toward you, communication is going to be difficult. Tell yourself that this is likely to be a temporary problem. If you were to believe it to be permanent, your belief would become a self-fulfilling prophecy.

How do you behave during this uncomfortable temporary period without going crazy? Here is an example of typical nonconversation

between a new partner and an eleven-year-old boy who was shy
and negative at the same time.

"I've got some hot chicken sandwiches for lunch, with french
fries. Would you like that, Freddy?"
"Okay."
"Do you want milk or Pepsi?"
"Okay."
"Which, Freddy?"
Silence. Freddy sighs, shrugs, goes to the fridge, opens it
and points to a bottle of Pepsi. He then closes the door and
goes back to the television set. His father switches off the set
and lets him have it.
"If you are asked a question, sir, you answer it. You say
'please' and you say 'thank you,' too."
"Okay, Dad."
Prolonged silence.

In the short term it doesn't matter much whether father intervenes or not. The result is still a stalemate as far as you and your
communication with Freddy are concerned.

If you recognize any of the elements of this nonconversation,
you may be relieved to know that you are by no means alone. You
are, in a nutshell, different from his mother; you are not an equal
alternative to her because he does not see you as often; he does
not know exactly how to relate to you, and, resenting this fact, he
resents you. All this the child tries to communicate to you by saying
as little as possible.

It helps for your partner to make it very clear to his child just
what is acceptable in terms of politeness and rudeness. But this
process can go too far if a child starts to associate you with being
told off. Get help from your partner, but don't use it as a crutch.
He cannot force communication to happen between you. If he tries
to, it will be at a considerable cost to his own standing with his
child. In the end, this is something you have to work out yourself—
with the child.

Among new partners, the best communicators seem to take a
good-natured view of obstacles thrown in their path. They regard

them as a challenge. But they do not make a fight out of it. They invent different kinds of approaches to suit the mood of the moment. They know instinctively that even a sad and worried child has a sense of humor. They play for that.

One woman is now on very good terms with her husband's twin boys. They talk to each other easily and naturally about practically anything at any time. There is a mood of good humor now, but it was not always like this. The first meetings were stiff and stilted. The twins, then seven, did not know what to make of her. They walked around her and avoided her questions. Noting that they felt more outgoing toward her dog, to the point of petting and feeding it, she got on all fours one day beside the dog, growled, and insisted, "Me too! Me too!" The twins roared with laughter. It was very hard for them to maintain the "ignoring game" after that. They became quiet with her again for a while. But when the time came to say good-bye, one of them grinned and patted her on the head. The following visit, after some uncertainty, they asked if she would play the dog game again.

The point of this account is not that this *particular* game actually worked, but that it is the *kind* of thing that can work. Should the twins have run from the kitchen when she went on all fours, there were any number of other things that she was prepared to try.

To get back to the hot-chicken-sandwich issue, which is a typical problem for the new partner, here is a scenario of how the humor principle can be applied:

> "I've got some hot chicken sandwiches for lunch. How does that grab you, Freddy?"
>
> "Okay."
>
> "Only okay? Which parts of the chicken would you like then, Freddy? The beak and the feet?"
>
> Freddy groans with a deprecating smile.
>
> "They're pretty good webbed feet, Freddy. Nice and chewy."
>
> Freddy turns away to his father. "I don't feel like lunch, Dad."
>
> "Maybe if you were a little more enthusiastic," says his father, "you might get a better sandwich. Go on, Freddy, ask Sally nicely."

With pursed lips, Freddy looks at Sally despite himself. "Please, Sally," he mumbles.

"Hm!" Sally rolls her eyes at him. " 'Please' takes you half-way down the gizzard, at least! I think the chicken's ready." Sally makes a clucking sound. "Does that sound ready to you?"

Freddy turns away in disgust. "That's for babies!"

"Bet you can't do better!"

Freddy starts to enjoy the kitchen at Sally's more than he likes to admit. He gives a superb rendition of a clucking chicken. He negotiates a mixture of dark and white meat. Sally gives him some gravy to check whether it's spicy enough. They have a funny argument about pepper.

Of course, this won't work every time. But looking for a humorous breakthrough will usually be far more rewarding than a frontal attack. In most cases you are very limited in the amount of time that you can actually spend with your partner's child: if each time there is a confrontation that is totally staid you have no chance to show that you are fun to talk to.

Humor needs some care. Avoid anything that seems to verge on teasing or sarcasm. As an adult, you could win at both very easily. But your aim is to encourage the child to relate to you because it is safe and fun to do so. Humor with an acid edge is neither safe nor fun.

You must also accept that this is a two-way street. Occasionally, yours may be a rueful smile. Your pride will be punctured by comic insults or practical jokes, which are often chosen as a symbolic way of getting back at you (not necessary you *personally*) for the fact that his parents split up. Can you laugh at yourself just a little?

Probably the biggest obstacles you will face are these:

1. Getting bored with trying. You are tired of meeting a brick wall, or of achieving a breakthrough only to have to start again from scratch the following week.

In this case, you should back off for a while. Leave most of the contact to your partner for a visit or two while you stay in the background. Try getting closer again in a few weeks, during a visit to some new place the three of you have not been to before.

2. Frustration at being taken for granted.

If you feel this way, avoid any explosive comments, like, "I'm not just the maid, you know!" Get your partner and his child to join you in the household chores or in anything that will serve as a reminder to everybody that if you tackle these things single-handedly, you deserve something in return. (If all else fails, organize a pizza strike: "What's for supper?" "Pizza. Here's the phone number. I'm off to my exercise class." It works.)

3. Ganging up, when there are two or more of them, and just one of you. Instead of talking with you they exchange glances, nudge each other, and giggle.

In this situation, you should look for ways in which to equalize the count for longer periods of time. Get your partner to agree that you should all four be doing things together more or separate the children occasionally for shopping expeditions, walks, work around the house, etc. One on one, you will find yourself getting on with each of them more easily.

Shyness sometimes disappears only when a person realizes that he can do something that is appreciated as useful and that makes him a minor hero for a moment or two. Try to involve him in the everyday life of the house. Being treated as a special guest is more likely to prolong shyness.

Jeanette

Jeanette felt she had no way of getting through to Jim at all. Her partner's son was fourteen when he first arrived at their house. He was taciturn, morose, unprepossessing, and suffered badly from acne. He didn't seem to fit in anywhere—even with the other teenage children that Jeanette once invited around. He was not very promising academically and seemed to have no particular talents.

Socially he was rather backward, as if he had decided at an early stage that he had better not trust anyone. When people talked to him, he often blushed; he seemed to prefer being left on his own. Even his father found he was hard to talk to.

Jeanette had hoped that Jim might show an interest in her two young children—aged three and one. But it was obvious that he found the small children more alarming than cute. He helped when he was required to, and was very little trouble. "But whenever he came into a room," Jeanette said, "he seemed to darken it."

Sometimes Jim's father had to be away on business, but Jim would still appear on the appointed weekends. This was partly his mother's choice, backed by his stepfather. These times were difficult for Jeanette. Neither clothes nor games meant much to him. Sports left him cold. Music he enjoyed, but only heavy metal, and Jeanette found that he could not really talk about music since listening to it for him meant shutting out the outside world. She gave him "watching duties"—supervising the young children and keeping an eye on whatever was cooking. But evenings were a problem.

One Saturday evening she left him to his own devices while she worked on a project in the basement. She needed to remove some tar patches from the surface of a wood floor. While scraping at them with an old knife, Jeanette was aware of a shadow across the floor in front of her. "You need glass," Jim told her. They split a cracked pane from an old storm window in the corner of the basement, and Jim proceeded to show how the operation should be done. Jeanette was grateful and told him so. He blushed furiously, but he was obviously satisfied. Jeanette asked him about the plans she had. Although he could never be classified as talkative, he was prepared to discuss practical details. Moreover, he seemed to like to do so, provided he was not cornered for too long.

Very gradually, using handyman questions as their main bridge, the two of them have been able to understand more about each other. Meanwhile, Jeanette has been able to open Jim's father's eyes to parts of Jim's character, and to the fact that he does in fact possess at least one valuable talent.

Another form of communication is one that many new partners avoid like the plague for as long as they can. Attitudes are admittedly changing faster, but chances are that you prefer not to have too much contact with your partner's ex-wife.

Where there is more than one ex-wife, there is apparently less of a problem. The main hang-ups occur when there has to be communication between just two women, an ex-wife and a current partner. Tension arises presumably because of the sense of rivalry in the background. Where the ex-wife has remarried or has a new partner, there tends to be less of a problem about communication, unless there is antagonism between the two males. You need to prepare yourself for this situation—it is something you cannot avoid altogether.

A sudden change of plan may put you on the telephone. Your partner is due to pick up his child at two o'clock. But at one o'clock he hasn't even got back to your home, let alone set out for his ex-wife's house. You call the airline and find that his flight has been delayed. You don't want the child and his mother to be hanging around waiting indefinitely, so you get in touch.

Alternatively, you may suddenly find yourself on the receiving end. A call is made to your home. Your partner is out. His ex-wife tells you that there has to be a change of plans because of sickness. You find yourself talking to her, taking notes, and discussing what new arrangement might be best.

Coping with this has made many of the women interviewed for this book grind their teeth. Yet it can be very straightforward, provided you follow some simple rules.

First, you should cultivate a *stance*. Choose one that seems to be right for you—right for your personality and for your feelings, primarily, but also right for the circumstances, and for what you know about your partner's ex-wife. The advantage is that you plan what to say, what to avoid saying, and how to get across the points you want to make. You are less likely to be flustered by the unexpected, and you can take barbed comments in your stride.

There are three main choices of stance; you can probably think of variations that might suit you more precisely.

1. "The Greek Messenger." This is the character in ancient tragedies whose job it is to announce news, usually bad. Because he is believed to be entirely on the sidelines, nobody would ever attack a Greek messenger. To play this role you deliberately choose an even and uninvolved tone of voice. You neither criticize nor defend. You talk about missed connections, lost clothing, or whatever, with regret but more or less without comment. Your effort goes into being on time, accurate, and helpful at taking and relaying messages. You never make a policy suggestion (for example, "Timmy should come around more often, I think."), and you duck the issue when asked for your opinion.

For someone who is by nature timid and apt to lose control in an emotional situation, this stance is right. However, you come across as a somewhat arid and possibly indifferent person. That is the trade-off.

2. "The Member of the Home Team." Here you identify totally with the hopes and fears of a tight-knit unit comprising yourself and your partner, and—when he is around—your partner's child. You are speaking more or less as an extension of your partner. You submerge your own doubts, if you have them, and express exactly what it is that you believe your partner would want you to be saying. This does not mean that you are prepared to trade insults or demand longer visits. That would be going beyond your role in the team. But you let your enthusiasm show through. ("So he'll be able to stay on another day with us, then? That's great! Thanks a million!") And you show disappointment. ("That's too bad that he can't stay long enough to watch the basketball game. They were both looking forward to it.")

You are not in the business of protesting decisions or attempting to persuade. The protesting and the persuasion is up to your partner. You are supporting his position. Wear the team colors clearly in each conversation you have.

In this stance you assume that the ex-wife will be looking at the child's visits as a desirable thing for all sides. This may not be so, but the assumption does no harm and may do some good. The fact that you obviously do care about the visits and what happens on the visits is important. With this stance you will encounter some resistance, perhaps some dislike, but you will probably generate some relief and possibly even some respect in the ex-wife's mind.

3. "The Voice of Reason." Sometimes a new partner sees that nothing but in-fighting takes place between her partner and his ex-wife when they are supposed to be working out details for visiting. The practical results are impossible schedules and children being taken to the beach without towels or swimming suits because they were told to expect a trip to the zoo. She feels a mediator is required, just for access. She takes over some of the communication, and is often more successful than either of the parents.

This stance requires skill. You will have to make each side feel that you really are pressing for concessions from the other. You need to avoid being drawn into anything emotional. You have to have a good eye for a compromise, and for the right moment to put together a deal.

Not every new partner can stand the strain that this stance involves. But unquestionably it is sometimes invaluable for maintaining contact between an absent parent and a child.

If, however, there is open warfare, you have very little hope. You are identified too easily with your partner to be an acceptable negotiator. But when the divorce battle is being fought in little skirmishes, there is a real need for a reasonable voice to say, "I do sympathize with that, and I will certainly pass on what you say. But meanwhile, is it okay if I drop by at ten o'clock to pick Annie up? I'll remember that you want her to get some new boots. And it was at four that you wanted her back this week, is that right?" This, of course, is not all. You then have to continue to your partner, "Well, dear, contrary to expectations we *will* be seeing Annie this weekend. Pick-up at ten, drop-off at four. Does that seem okay? I *know* I can't get any extension. Now, are you ready for the curve ball? Do you remember those pink boots we saw? You don't? Well, do you think we can afford them? They're about twelve dollars. . . ."

To fulfill this role demands time and a thick skin, too, particularly in the early stages. A business background helps—for example, in telephone selling or in real estate. Those who perform this role regularly get a lot of satisfaction. In some cases, if it had not been for their negotiating skills, all contact between father and child would have broken down.

Once you decide which of these roles is going to be "you," the sudden call will not find you unprepared. Try not to change your stance too frequently. If you do, you risk being seen as unreliable.

The telephone is going to be your main means of communication, whichever stance you adopt. Here are some guidelines:

1. If you have a tough call to make to your partner's ex-wife, get it over with as quickly as you reasonably can. Allow yourself fifteen minutes to decide what to say, then make the call. Never delay.

2. If you feel that you have said the wrong thing on the telephone, call back immediately. Even if it is just to say, "I may have given you the wrong impression just now, that I'm not looking forward to Annie's visit. I just want to say that I'm looking forward to it very much." Act quickly. Never brood on these things.

3. If she is calling *you*, always sound pleased to hear from her, regardless of your real feelings. It gives you a better sense of being in control, as opposed to being caught off guard. If the rest of the conversation can be kept on the same pleasant level, you have scored a victory for civilization, too.

4. Early in the conversation, ask how she is. If you can remember something about which she was concerned, ask about that, too. You should also ask after your partner's child. Apart from being more agreeable, this gives you some time to think.

5. At this point, ask if it is you that she wants to talk to, or your partner. Should her child be staying with you at this time, you should, of course, offer to call him to the phone.

6. There are a number of issues she could raise that are best left

to your partner. Just say, politely, "I see what you mean. I'll talk to Jack about that—but it's really up to him to decide." These issues include major changes in the visiting schedule and anything to do with money.

7. If there is criticism of anything like your status vis-à-vis your partner, the way you bring up your children, or particular incidents reported back by her child, the rule is *not* to allow yourself to be drawn into an emotional argument. You are less concerned about self-defense than about the contact between your partner and his child. For this you must keep things cool.

There are several useful ploys which can help achieve this. Use phrases like "I hear what you say, but I do feel you are exaggerating"; "You know, that has occurred to me, too, but then . . ." and change the subject. Or, you can alter the course of the argument suddenly (for example, "from Annie's point of view, what she really seems to enjoy when she comes here is . . ." and continue any way that you please). You might also recall some remark made by the ex-wife in your last conversation with her ("Do you know, that's reminded me of something you said last time that really made me think. What was it? Something about . . ."); if you get it wrong, she will correct you, but the subject has effectively been changed. It is best to rehearse some closing lines calculated to end the conversation quickly but politely. ("Isn't it difficult trying to live in the 1980s? The ground rules are getting fewer. But Annie's smile when she sees Jack again makes it seem worth working out.")

8. If there is sarcasm or an accusation in her voice, avoid replying in kind. You could probably burn her ears off if you wanted, but that would win one battle at the cost of the war. Just be true to your stance. You may occasionally give a short laugh and say, "That was a good one!" This is remarkably disarming. So is "Wow! You're so much quicker than me." But go very easy on this. Avoid elaborate comments like asking if she is in collaboration with Neil Simon or Edward Albee—that kind of thing has all been said before, many times. If you can rescue

the communication from this level, you will be achieving something substantial.

9. If she makes an attack on your partner, defend him quietly: "Oh, I'm sure that's not what Jack intended," and change the subject. Sometimes there will be a compulsion to draw you into a discussion about him, for example, "By the way, how's he getting on with his drinking problem, or should I say how's the drinking problem getting on with *him*?" This remark took one new partner so much by surprise that she became incoherent and had to endure mocking laughter and the closing line, "I think you've told me all I need to know—but try to keep it down when the kids are over there, will you?" A simple way out of such a situation is a curt "I'll ask him." Nothing more is necessary.

10. If the receiver is slammed down at the other end, resist the temptation to do the same yourself. If this happens before you have gotten essential information for a forthcoming visit, call her back up right away. Start with "Hello, I believe we were cut off." Then go straight to the details.

11. When you are calling *her* and somebody else answers, ask if you can talk to her directly. Avoid making use of her partner or her child as a convenient go-between. Many parents resent this.

Some people prefer expressing themselves in letters, even inside the city limits. If you do this, you must allow at least a day longer for delivery than you would expect. Have your partner check the letter before mailing it, simply to see if anything is ambiguous: if an arrangement for meeting a child can in any way be misinterpreted, then it most surely will be.

There are some circumstances in which you really have to use the telephone, and use it quickly. These include accidents, serious illnesses, and any incidents that have attracted the attention of the police. Ask yourself, is this a situation which I, as a mother, would prefer to be told about immediately? Something like a fall from a tree, followed by a trip to the hospital to check out a suspected fracture, would almost certainly qualify. In some of these situations you may well ask, "Why me?" It would be perfectly possible for your partner to call instead of you. But that may not always be possible. Sometimes he may be too emotionally shaken to make a practical and objective call. In some cases, too, particularly if you have children of your own, you may be able to communicate and discuss symptoms more effectively with the child's mother than he can.

While it makes sense, when possible, to bring the child to the telephone during the conversation, the initial part of the call should be outside the range of the child's voice. It is extremely bad for any mother to be told that everything is going to be all right while she can hear her child crying, screaming, or throwing up in the background.

Not all communication is unpleasant where the ex-wife is concerned. After a while, you may find that being pleasant on the telephone, and above all practical and understanding, pays off. You will then have a pleasant acquaintance with whom to deal. Many ex-spouses nowadays meet at regular intervals, together with their new partners, to talk about their children and what they feel about their children's development so that their parenting efforts can be more compatible. This could happen to you, allowing you to be less concerned about your stance and more natural in your communication.

Possibly your most difficult communication task is going to be not with the child or his mother, but with your own partner. Perhaps not now, but later. The subject will be his relationship with his child, when something seems to you to be going wrong.

You will probably be able to sense that your partner needs support to be able to admit that something is wrong. There may be a number of questions in his mind:

1. Is it all worthwhile? I'm seeing my child regularly, but I don't feel closer to him; he seems bored; he likes money and treats more than he likes me; he doesn't think too much of me; his values are very different from mine.

2. Is there some kind of permanent effect that the marriage breakup has had, and is continuing to have, on this child? Will it get worse? Will he be disturbed? Antisocial? Unable to develop his talents?

3. What exactly is the cost of all this visiting on my present relationship with my partner? And with our own children? Am I neglecting her and our children? What is the effect on her— short-term and long-term?

Some of this you may judge to be too sensitive to bring fully into the open. But if you suspect that your partner is worried, you will help him if you can encourage him to discuss these problems in a calm way. Do so on an *occasional* basis: there is no point in digging up a plant every week to examine its roots. Ask positive questions—questions rather than comments, since it is after all *his* child you are talking about. After a weekend visit, a positive way to start a conversation might be:

> "Well, that wasn't so bad, was it? Both the kids seemed to enjoy that a lot."
>
> Then: "Are they more mature now, or am I just imagining it? Do you feel that way about them now?"
>
> And probe, if necessary: "What struck you most of all about them this time? See if it's the same thing that struck me . . ."
>
> Later: "Where do you think they are going, in fact? What do you think they will be like when they get there?"

Obviously you will have some thoughts of your own to contribute during this, but the main task is to get his doubts, whatever they are, voiced so that they can be looked at rather than just suppressed. (A negative lead-in might be something like this: "Well, there they go again! They certainly seemed to enjoy that, but I'm not so sure about us." This is more likely to make a father clam up than start to talk and reappraise what's going on.)

However gloomy you yourself may feel about his children, there is little point in being negative about them unless you have something positive to offer as a suggestion. Think of ideas for new things to do during visits. Make a list of interests from an advertisement for night classes, and prepare another list of household projects that could involve everybody (a painting weekend, a basement-clearing operation, a spring attack on the garden). Take a look at local voluntary projects and see if the family could help on one of them, even on just an occasional basis. If you keep a number of ideas ready to pass to your partner at appropriate moments, he is likely to think more positively himself about being a Saturday parent, and he, too, will be less of a slave to routine.

Being the provider of ideas puts you in an excellent position for airing legitimate complaints. Typically, these will be concerned with the extra housework that the visits involve, together with the loss of your own free weekend time, and perhaps of time you could be spending with your own children. You *must* say when these are getting to be important issues—preferably before they become serious. If you participate in the planning of your partner's children's visits, you will find them all the easier.

9 : Your Own Children

It is not uncommon nowadays in new partnerships that each partner has either custody of or rights of access to children by their first marriage. In either case, there are now two sets of children to consider, rather than one. The new partnership may create more children, too. A key problem arises when your children from your earlier marriage are brought into contact with your partner and his children.

Look at it from the point of view of your partner's child, who may be a regular or a very occasional visitor. If he is used to seeing his father, he values this. Now there are new people to consider: first there is yourself, who is obviously somebody very dear to his father, and then there is a child who also obviously means something to him. Especially if your own child is living permanently with you and with his father, your partner's child may be prone to this pattern of thought:

> Instead of just seeing me, my father is seeing this woman, too, when we meet. She is with him more of the time than I am because she is around when I leave. She has control over much of the house. She has a child, too, who seems better settled into the house than I am. I must struggle to have a lot of time with my father, to have some time alone with him, and to say things to him without having to look over my shoulder. Somehow I've got to stay number one with him.

If the struggle seems unequal, he may continue in this vein:

> I just don't like this arrangement. I should show everybody
> how much I dislike it. Maybe Dad will get the idea, and pitch
> these other people out.

This may seem rather a hard line for a child to take. He is unlikely to put these thoughts together consciously; he is more likely to have fantasies in which he seizes his father's attention by proving smarter than the rest, punishes his father for disloyalty, and eclipses yourself and your child. Part of him wants to relive a previous era, when both his parents were together. Whether they all had a good time or not doesn't matter—the new world seems more threatening. What is going to be permanent, and what is merely transitional? One anchor that he may have relied on was contact with his father. Now, suddenly, there is competition. The anchor may be less permanent than he had supposed.

Moreover, your own child has begun enjoying the closeness of a home with a mother and a father. Your partner's child's mother may have a new partner herself, and if that is accepted happily by him, this point will rankle much less. But if he is a one-parent child and perceives your child as having two parents, some jealousy is obviously to be expected.

In a family that grows up together there is time to be prepared for the arrival of a new brother or sister. This is not the case when two older children are thrown together for the first time. It will be different, and usually much easier, if you and your partner decide to start a family together. You can then share some of the preliminary excitement with your partner's child. At the very least he will have suggestions for the baby's name. But when the competition appears ready made, with some hints of a relationship already forming between his father and this new child, it is quite natural to feel threatened.

This sense of threat will be all the greater if:

1. Your partner's child is making only occasional, brief visits, while your child is resident either permanently or on an extended basis (as in joint custody).
2. Your partner's child has come to depend on a pattern or rhythm to his visits (especially between the ages of six and nine) and this pattern is changed.
3. Your own child has his own "territory" in your home, while your partner's child does not feel that any space belongs to him. This is especially painful if you and your child have moved in with his father, and your child has taken over what he previously regarded as his own territory.
4. Your own child and your partner get on extremely well, and are demonstratively affectionate with each other.
5. Your own child has some kind of superiority—real or perceived—that is felt to give him an advantage in your partner's esteem and affection.

THE INFLUENCE OF AGE DIFFERENCE
ON CHILDREN'S INTERACTION

For simplicity's sake I have assumed that both are only children. Brothers and sisters, of course, change the picture. As a general rule, an only child is more sensitive about loss of time with his parent because of another child being there, because he has less experience of sharing on a day-to-day basis.

Age is by no means the only factor. Personality differences will result in two visiting children of identical ages reacting to the same resident child in different ways. One child may be more outgoing and more self-confident. He will feel that he can handle the competition, and that this might be fun, too. The other child may be more cautious, defensive, and unwilling to see anything other than a war of attrition.

For reasons of space, a male child has been assumed. But the same principles apply to both boys and girls. However, there are two main points about gender to keep in mind. First (mainly because of social conditioning), more girls than boys will find something very appealing in a child who is younger than they are. (But do not assume that all girls will take a delighted interest in a child under five: many will run a mile to get away.) Second, there does seem to be some reduction of competition when your partner's child and your child are of opposite sexes.

1. If your partner's child is under three years old and your child is the same age, your partner's child may react with indifference—except for special moments, such as when your partner picks up your child, or feeds him, or rocks him to sleep. If your child is a little older your partner's child may react with awe, and perhaps inferiority, since your child seems so big, strong, mobile, and skillful by comparison. If your child is four or more years older, there may still be awe, but indifference, too, if your child keeps away from him; not much sense of competition; a liking for his attention, perhaps, if your child shows an interest in him, offers treats, etc.

2. If your partner's child is three to five years old and your child is younger, there may be strong jealousy if your partner looks after your child too much. This can be deflected if he is encouraged to help with "the baby," but he must be supervised closely. If your child is the same age, there may be rivalry, a desire to show off and to prove superiority; distrust may delay playing together—when this play comes it will be stormy but valuable as a tension reliever; they learn that they benefit from one another. If your child is a little older, your partner's child may show resentment, a desire for his father to repudiate your child, since he feels inadequate to compete directly; complaints of unfairness and being hurt are likely to be common. If your child is four or more years older there may still be resentment if your child enjoys taking center stage in the family, or in bossing. If your child keeps more to himself, to you, and to his friends, he is less of a threat.

3. If your partner's child is six to eight years old and your child is under three, your partner's child may show irritation with your child as a source of disturbance, rather than alarm at a direct competitor; curiosity and pleasure at helping look after him, if you treat the older child as responsible. If your child is three to five years old, your partner's child may react with suspicion, especially when he observes his father treating your child as he himself used to be treated until recently (for example, being bathed, carried, or fed); some aggression can be expected, either direct (pushing, shouting) or indirect (teasing, criticizing); some regression, too (acting as if at a younger age, when more attention was given him).

If your child is the same age, your partner's child will be very competitive; anxious to compare academic or athletic achievements, skills at games, knowledge of riddles or swear words—anything to measure progress. Neither he nor your child will want any weakness to show in front of you or your partner. There will be plenty of tears, if either party loses face for an instant. (They may get along better when neither of you are known to be watching.)

If your child is nine to twelve years old, your partner's child may be impressed by the older child's knowledge of the world and growing independence of spirit, which make fewer demands on your partner's time. This may decrease competitiveness. If your child is four or more years older, he will be out of reach, and will be judged much more on his own merits than in terms of the competition he represents.

4. If your partner's child is nine to twelve years old and your child is under three, your partner's child will be unlikely to see much of a threat, except perhaps in financial terms. Your child will be seen as cute, but a nuisance. If your child is three to five years old, your partner's child may react with annoyance, because a younger child can play attention-winning games more than an older child would be expected to. He may get frustrated, even aggressive.

If your child is six to eight years old, your partner's child may still show annoyance, but will have more confidence in being able to outwit a child who is just a bit younger. Aware that he probably impresses the younger child, he may become more of a brother. If your child is the same age, it is unlikely that your child is as much in need of your partner's approval at this age, and there may be less competitive tension. *But* in the unusual case that your child has found his perfect father figure in your partner (if, for example, he has not seen his own father for a long time), there may be a battle royal for love and attention, with no holds barred. This combination of ages is likely to be a good one, but it is also capable of being the worst in terms of fighting.

If your child is older, he will be relating more and more to his friends, and treating his parents' house as a home base. Your partner's child is less likely to feel under pressure in his relationship with his father. Exceptions come when the father is obviously very much in admiration of the older child, and is prone to make comparisons.

5. If your partner's child is thirteen to fifteen years old and your child is under six, pubertal interest in babies may outweigh all else. But a young teen will demand "quality time," allowing for discussion of his problems, joint expeditions of a more adult kind, a chance to show off his increasing maturity, etc. Expect resentment, then, if at weekends the whole world seems to revolve around the nursery.

If your child is six to eight years old, your partner's child may be flattered by your child's admiration into accepting the role of older brother, but will want some time, if just a short while, alone with his father. If your child follows him everywhere, there may be trouble. If your child is nine to twelve years old, this combination may work well, since both have more understanding of their need to have contact with each of you.

If your child is the same age, the possibilities of friendship between the two children will tend to outweigh the drive to compete. The two are mature enough to compare notes, and will probably swap life histories if they like each other at least a little. Comparisons will be made, however, at a more sophisticated level, just to see whether one is getting a better "deal" (for example, when one gets a calculator for a gift, and the other a camera, they will ponder the hidden message in this difference).

If your child is sixteen or older, there should not be too much of a problem, provided their personalities are reasonably compatible, at least as far as relations with your partner are concerned.

Regardless of your child's age, if your partner's child is sixteen or older, the big question in his mind is going to be, "Am I going to be forgotten by my father now that he has this other, younger family around him?" His sensitivity on this issue depends partly on how close the two have been over the years and partly on how far he has progressed toward becoming an independent adult in his own right. If there is a younger member of your family (say, under nine) who welcomes some attention from an older teenager, this may help since it provides a reason for hanging around when not actually doing something with his father. If he is still very dependent, a role in your home such as "uncle" to a younger child may be necessary.

Sometimes you will find that the patterns just described do not fit the facts. Another important factor may be coming into play. This is the specific experience that your partner's child may have had before. When he comes to visit his father and finds your child there, he may be reminded of something: for example, when your partner had another second partner, before he met you; or when his mother introduced him to the children of *her* new partner. Such encounters may have been pleasant or unpleasant. Possibly nobody knows about this except the child himself. It is the kind of thing that can cast a long shadow.

Certainly not all aspects of the relations between the children are tied to competitiveness for your partner's attention. Other considerations weigh heavily, too. Among children under six, there may be a fear of these new people and what they might do (Are they keeping Daddy against his will? Might they do the same to me?) and fear of the strange new house (What are those odd noises?). Meanwhile, children above age six may experience jealousy—sometimes of possessions, but mainly of skills and other attainments, including popularity. This is not unconnected, as a rule, with jealousy of the ability to secure attention and approval. You may need to encourage your partner to notice more often the minor attainments of his child, especially if they are in danger of being overshadowed by those of your own child. (The opposite should obviously apply, too.)

Whichever age groups you are dealing with, and however many children are involved, the major rule has to be this: justice not only should be done, but it should also be perceived. Children will make comparisons of the ways in which they get treated, however much you discourage it. This happens among brothers and sisters in most "normal" families, and it is much more likely in families where children are suddenly thrown together.

"Equal" presents are not always possible. Different age groups want different things costing different amounts. Older children sometimes visit stores to check whether the gift they received is at least as valuable as that received by their father's partner's child. When children live together all the time, the presents they receive have less impact on their sense of who is getting priority. With two children who are based in different houses, you have to be more careful. It helps a great deal to include a child in the planning, purchase, or wrapping of the present for the "rival" child, since this gives him the feeling of being closer to key decisions.

The same point applies to other areas. Try to get *both* children (not necessarily at the same time) involved in talking about an upcoming trip or vacation. You can ask each one questions about what clothes or food the other prefers. This way you increase the feeling that each child is being accepted. It is a process that should never stop. One simple case history illustrates this point:

Greta
Carl, aged ten, lived with his mother, Greta, and her new partner, Ian. Hannah, Ian's daughter, also aged ten, visited occasionally for weekends, and for a week of the summer vacation. This particular vacation was at the beach. Early in the week both children were told they could have a souvenir to take home at the vacation's end. "That establishes equality," Greta thought to herself. But halfway through the week Hannah left her watch on the beach and

the tide removed it. She was very unhappy about it, and Greta offered to replace the watch at the end of the week.

With feigned unconcern, Carl immediately wanted to know if she would be getting the watch as well as a souvenir. A problem arose when, simultaneously, Greta said no and Ian said yes. Ian felt it would be unfair to Hannah not to have a souvenir as well, since she would merely be going away with what she had already owned on arrival. Greta's thinking had been that they could get Hannah a better watch on their way back: this would surely please her and make her feel that she had got something special out of the vacation. Greta was concerned about money while Ian was more anxious to be equally generous to both children.

Over the next few days the children tried various ways of finding out who would get what, and what it would cost. Greta and Ian put off making a decision.

Relations between the two children got worse. Carl wanted to know when he might expect to have a watch of his own. He and Hannah criticized each other, told tales, sought out different companions on the beach, and tried to persuade whomever they found not to play with their rival.

In the end, the partners agreed that the issue had grown out of all proportion. Already two days had been spoiled by sullen looks, fighting, and short tempers. To rescue the vacation Greta persuaded Ian to adopt the following plan. They would all go to the shop immediately and buy two identical watches, cheaper than the one Greta had originally thought of, with wrist bands of different colors, and two souvenir wooden sailboats, with hulls of different colors. It was explained that Hannah was getting a watch to replace the one she had lost, while Carl was getting one because he did not own one, but had been promised one sometime ago. This reasoning seemed to go down well.

Relations improved, but there was always a tendency for the children to glance over their shoulders to make sure there was no favoritism.

Note that the low point in Greta's story, as far as the children are concerned, occurred when the partners were in open conflict:

the children feared that each partner might favor his own child if the issue were not carefully policed. Delaying agreement between the partners does not help. When there has been a dispute of this kind, a decision needs to be made by the parents together, and communicated firmly to the children at once: the children at this point are usually too agitated to participate constructively in the decision-making process.

No child should get priority treatment over anther. Theoretically, the children from both sides should be equals, with equal rights. But it does not always work out that way. Some children know exactly what they want and they make sure that they get it. When they get an idea, they push hard for it and they generally get their way; other children in the same circumstances are more passive. Most children have known a more dominant child at some time during their childhood: this was the personality who decided what the next game would be, when they would leave the yard and head for the corner store, what they should feel toward other groups of children. This experience is not limited to a few extreme examples: in every home where there are children, usually there is one who is a bit quicker to demand the easiest of a set of chores, to state unequivocally what he wants for Christmas, and to get help with his homework.

The chances are, in fact, that you will *not* find a perfect balance between children. One will be a little more inclined to suggest, another will more often take suggestions. There may be certain times when they reverse roles, but there will probably be an overall pattern of one acting and the other being acted upon.

New partners are often unrealistic in expecting children to exchange turns religiously, or to share any little advantage they might have. There is nothing wrong about having some ideals with regard to sharing and mutual respect. But each is an individual, and will be looking out for his own interests.

Keep a sharp lookout during the first few encounters for any really serious imbalances between the children. They will *not* be perfect angels in their relations with each other. But they should not be allowed to get away with bullying, persistent teasing, making sure the weaker one always gets the worst deal, ganging up (especially when there are two children on one side and only one on the other), seizing or breaking the other's possessions, or crowding the weaker child out of conversations, parental attention, and joint activities. It is the flagrant injustices you should concentrate on, when these seem likely to create a set pattern of imbalance if they are unchecked. Isolated instances of aggression or unpleasantness are less of a concern—everybody has bad days. Just make sure that no child is consistently made to feel inferior or unhappy.

The first few encounters are important because it is only then that you have a chance of changing something that starts badly. Children will typically work out a sort of pecking order among themselves. If that order seems too rigid or too cruel, step in quickly. Talk to your partner about it as soon as you can. Separate the children before the visit ends, if possible. Decide jointly with your partner what exactly is going wrong, and remember that his perception of it may be different from yours. Then talk to the children, both of you, to try to head things off. The weaker child, particularly one coming in from the outside, needs to be shown that there is law and order in your home. Otherwise he will cling to his parent, if he can, which probably will make his relations with the other children even worse. From this point, he will need for the most part to fight his own battles. If you are intervening all the time, nobody benefits.

If behavior between the children gets progressively worse, the first rule is still to talk to your partner and discuss what is wrong. Short visits can be made more pleasant simply by giving the children less time together. Longer visits from your partner's child, however, are more difficult to manage in this way. It is important not to make either child feel that he is being deprived of the company of either of you because of bad behavior or inadequacy. Try to arrange for the children to pursue different interests: avoid situations where both are fishing in the same boat, using the same bait, tangling each other's lines, criticizing each other's technique. If there is a sense of inferiority setting in for one child, he needs to be given a clear chance to develop a talent of his own to help increase his confidence in your home. Maybe he could be the one to go to riding lessons, skating lessons, music class, or a theater group. The essential thing is to let the child in the weaker position compete in an arena different from the one with all the lions in it, even just for a while.

When you are striving for harmony between warring sets of kids, you are trying to avoid one child associating another with difficulty (real or imagined) at getting through to his own parent.

Gerda

Gerda and Tony began living together on a trial basis. She was divorced, with joint custody of her two children, Gavin and Edwina. He was separated, and met with his two children, Clare and Richard, every other Sunday. There were then two semiresident children, and two who were occasional visitors. Their ages had a lot to do with how they got on with each other.

Both Gavin and Clare were fifteen. They had totally divergent interests. Gavin played every sport he could possibly cram into a fifty-two week year. When he wasn't playing, he was thinking and talking about sports. Clare was unathletic, noncompetitive, and had been encouraged in her home to make things like rugs, dolls, clothes, and cakes. There was very little conversation between them. They kept out of each other's way. She called him a jock, and he called her weird. But they tolerated each other with very few problems. Two years later, they like each other, despite not having anything in common. They had never had any doubts that each could see and talk to Tony as much as they wanted, even when both were in the house at the same time.

Edwina was eleven and Richard was five. Neither child had adjusted as well as the two older ones to their parents' separations. Edwina wanted more time with her mother, and was protesting the joint-custody arrangement. Richard was going through a series of different moods: sometimes he was aggressive with his father, blaming him for going away, while at other times he would show off as if he were indifferent to it all. He was alternately very jealous of his sister Clare and very dependent on her.

When Richard arrived, Edwina thought he looked cute, and that it might be nice to treat him as a baby brother. But Richard rejected this role outright. He was more anxious to get as much time with his father as he could, or failing that, with Clare. Edwina he saw as someone who was always getting in his way, keeping him from his father. When he was not actually with Tony, Richard was usually running around the house, making a lot of noise, getting into everything that he shouldn't. He needed a lot of supervision.

At first just to defend her home, but more and more because she felt Richard was a sad child who needed help, Gerda gave him a lot of her time. So did his father, when he could. In fact Richard succeeded in taking most of the parental attention away from the other children. This left Edwina feeling pushed into a corner. She decided she hated Richard.

The first long weekend they all shared together was a memorable one. Richard found that if he accused Edwina of pinching and hitting him, and if he cried loudly enough, Gerda or Tony would comfort him and tell Edwina off. (Exactly how much provocation there might have been is uncertain, but it gradually became apparent that Edwina was more sinned against than sinning.) By Sunday afternoon she exploded and told Tony, "Your brat is a bloody little liar!" She ran weeping from the house, in the general direction of her father's home. Gerda followed her, had a long walk with her, and persuaded her to return. She apologized. But the end of the weekend came as a relief.

Reconstruction of a reasonable atmosphere was long and rather painful. When children do not see each other very often and they have had a serious dispute, they tend to stick at the same point. If they have more points of contact they can adapt their impressions of each other more easily.

Gerda and Tony helped each child plan something separately or with friends for at least part of the weekend when the visiting children were to arrive. Each, that is, except Richard. Tony had to spend more of the weekend exclusively with him, taking him to a swimming pool, a playing field, or anywhere that would get him exhausted while satisfying his need to be with his father.

Dividing a family up seems a strange and rather unfortunate way to aim at better harmony. But here the children's best interests, personalities, and concerns were very different. Tony would have liked to spend more time with Clare. But Richard was at a stage where he clearly needed the most help, and tying Clare's time down to Richard's needs and preventing her from doing what she wanted was not an appealing idea. Gerda tried, with some success, to organize outings that she could undertake with Clare and Edwina together, but the age gap between the two girls often meant that a compromise had to be reached on the kinds of activity they pursued. In addition, it was not very satisfying from Gerda's point of view that the male and female members of the family should always be separated.

Reconstructing the family life took a long time. But as the two younger children grew more accustomed to the way their lives were organized and had more confidence in their close relationships with both their parents, they became easier to live with. It would be stretching the truth to say they were friendly with each other, but they were no longer antagonistic. The most difficult rift to heal was between Edwina and Tony—their pride was too much involved.

A possible way of improving their situation would have been for Gerda's children to visit their father whenever Tony's came to visit. But this idea did not appeal much when they had thought it over. It seemed too much like an admission of defeat, like telling one set of children they must get out because the others are due in. Even in families where space is very limited, parents seem to prefer their children to meet together when possible: even where there is some incompatibility, life seems happier this way.

Be optimistic at the start, and let the children find out about each other in a natural way. But observe those first encounters in case danger signals arise: don't ignore persistent signals, or there will be trouble, as between Edwina and Richard. If you try to make sure that each feels he is getting a fair share of the good things, the danger signals may soon disappear. But, if necessary, be prepared to divide your forces (you and your partner) along whatever lines seem right. Then you can decide when to regroup and try again.

Preferential treatment can include discipline. If you are to stand a chance of healing the relations between two sets of children, it is crucial that each feels that neither of them can get away with more than the other. (This may have been just a perceptual problem where Edwina was concerned. But it was a very real problem to *her*.)

The same applies to privileges. Children are bound to notice if only one is allowed to watch late television shows, leave his homework earlier, or have the first pick of the chores. Since they are naturally competitive, they may complain even about matters of chance, such as one sitting next to the driver more often during a weekend than the other, or one sitting on a knee and the other on a chair during story-telling time. Again, it is the children's perception, not the reality, that matters. It may be irritating to accommodate their perception of what fairness means, but it is very important if they are to feel secure with each other.

You may have found one family a handful—wait until you try two! Nonetheless, the accounts of children getting together and enriching each other's and their parents' lives certainly outweigh the disaster stories. Throughout all the false starts and the long reconstructions, the strength of character of the new partner who observes carefully what each child seems to need as an individual, and who works actively with her partner to achieve a sense of fairness, usually establishes a happy home in the end.

10 : If You Are the Male Partner

As the male partner, you may or may not have your own child, but you are living with or regularly visiting a woman whose child is in his father's custody and makes periodic visits. Your partner wants to keep up whatever contact she can with her child, and your aim is to help her.

You will almost certainly face one problem at some point or other in a more intense form than will your female counterparts. Although society is often liable to criticize a father who is living apart from his child, this eases up with time. If he maintains a good relationship with his child, people are ready to give him some credit for this. However, when it is the mother who is absent, there is a much stronger tendency for others to lay a guilt trip on her. This may pursue her long after she has shown that she is capable of helping her child with consistent contact. This means that she needs a lot of help from you.

One man in your situation clearly recalls what used to happen every other weekend. He always drove to the corner of the block where her son lived, because the mother was too nervous to drive. At this point she took over the wheel for two hundred yards. Meanwhile, he waited in the doorway of a cigar store. (The ex-husband, long after he had remarried, was known to become enraged if he so much as caught sight of the new partner.)

When the mother walked up the drive to the door of the house, she would see the door open just a quarter of the way, so that no visual contact would take place between her and her ex-husband. "C'mon, Johnny," the father's voice would say, "it's your . . . mother." There was always the same pause between "your" and "mother." Some two years after this process had begun, she was surprised one weekend to see that the door opened about halfway. An elderly woman's face appeared, and scrutinized her. This was the father's new wife's mother. The second time this happened, Johnny's mother smiled and said, "Hello." The reply was an outraged "How could you?"

The new male partner had to be very supportive, over a long period of time.

Not all visiting arrangements are as highly charged with emotion as this one. But to be realistic you must expect the occasional pointing finger.

Sometimes this affects the relationship between the mother and child, too. Unfortunately, children are sometimes told that their mother is "not a very good mother," or even that she "did you a bad turn." This is bad for their own self-esteem, and undermines the pleasure they otherwise get from regular visits. Some of society's signals to a child caught in this circumstance are that he should continue to punish his mother—to complain to her, be aggressive to her, be critical of the things she does—for quite some time (longer, certainly, than in the case of an absent father).

When you are watching your partner's child during these visits, it is worth considering that if he misbehaves, he is in part responding to the signals he gets from those around him. These come from school as well as from relatives and neighbors. While children from split families are already in the majority in many classrooms, it is still a little unusual for a child to be living with his father rather than with his mother. Joint custody is beginning to change that, but a child not living with his mother still attracts attention, not all of it kind. "His mother walked out on him" is occasionally heard.

There are some positive steps that you can take to help correct any bad impressions. The first is to build up his mother in the child's eyes. After that, it is a question of trying to keep her in his high regard. At the same time, you can point out to him how much his mother loves him. These tasks are very important for you and your new family: nobody else can help in quite the same way. How you go about it is important, too. If you push too far, going over his mother's virtues again and again and repeating how much she has been missing her child, you are liable to achieve the opposite effect from what you intend. Most of the time, you simply have to be entirely natural. But just occasionally, give her a compliment right out loud. Give the child a smile and say, "Oh, she loves you so much!"—just occasionally, it means a lot. (If you are overdoing it, you can usually tell because the child will look around the room for the escape hatch.)

Expressing the fact that you admire someone is at its most natural and its most convincing when you are simply talking and listening. It is expressed in the way that you ask for information or for an opinion, and the way you listen to it. You argue, sure, but with mutual respect. Respect for his mother is perhaps the most crucial feeling that you can show her child.

From a negative point of view, you express a high regard for her by not putting her down, by laughing with her and not at her. Maybe your new partner is not the world's best driver, or cook, or household economist, or bridge partner, or whatever: but in front of her child is not the place to point this out.

If you have children of your own, particularly if they are living with you, help your partner make it clear to her child that it was not in order to change children that she came to live with you. Her own child is still very special. You can help make this more apparent if you: describe occasions when you have gone shopping together to look for something for her child; ask after illnesses, making it clear that both you and his mother were worried about them and are following what is going on; describe situations in which the child's name came up between you and she wondered what her child was doing just then; avoid tactless remarks, particularly when her child is not feeling on top of the world, about how much his mother admires your own children.

There is an easy and convenient way of showing that you care even when her child is not there. This is keeping a little picture gallery devoted to the good times you have shared with the child— it is fun, and he can contribute to it. All you require is a little space on a wall and a two-foot-square bulletin board. Pin up a selection of photos, car stickers showing where you have been together, programs from sports events or shows, or little drawings or messages received from the child. The mother should organize the gallery, but she should allow you and the child to help. Eventually the child may take over, showing that this is something he regards as very important.

One family I visited had a whole wall in the basement devoted to mementos of this kind. This was known as "Jack and Linda's wall." The idea had first occurred to their mother. It was put into practice by her new partner, who resurfaced the wall to receive pegs, stickers, and pins. There were pictures, fishing tackle, pennants, a hockey puck, old ballet shoes, school-theater programs, homemade puppets, clay models, a rattlesnake's rattle mounted on a board proclaiming "Mojave Desert," hand-prints of the children taken at different times, and more. Each of these items had some commemorative value; in total they summed up a history of contact of which the family was proud.

The advantage of having a large-scale "memory bank" is that the children can join in easily. They like looking for new items. Sometimes they make them themselves. It is not a museum so much as a living memory bank that mother and child build on an ongoing basis. Children notice the interest and the love that go into putting it together. They are very observant of any changes that take place.

If you agree to the principle of having such a space, if you help in its construction, *and* if you keep it free from depredations of your own child, you have already done a lot. Make suggestions about what might go on it, but keep your distance. It is primarily *theirs*.

Many of the new male partners interviewed said that they had had problems over discipline. They made an inteesting point that is specific to this chapter: that it would "all have been easier" if the child had been coming over to see his father instead of his mother. The point they make is that there is a stronger taboo against a man interfering or imposing discipline when the child is visiting his mother.

In addition to sensing that they should not "interfere," these new male partners evidently felt it was wrong even to complain to their partners when they profoundly disagreed with what the children were being allowed to get away with. By the time they talked frankly, the visit was practically over. Some of them never got talking at all. Everything was festering and rankling, resulting in a rather embittered (although not always totally negative) attitude toward the child himself, and a compulsion to talk to an outside interviewer about how bad things had been.

Often they seemed to bottle up their feelings for too long. By the time they talked there was already disagreement about what had actually happened, and no clear plan evolved for what they would do differently next time. This stems from sheer love for the mother and a regard for her emotions where the child is concerned. You do not, they seemed to be saying, kick a mother when she is down—and particularly not *this* mother. But there is some resentment of the child as a complicating factor, a nuisance, a potential threat to developing one's own family with this wonderful woman.

Tell your partner exactly what you feel about what is happening in your house. Overprotection by not communicating frankly is harmful in the long run. Assuming you have met your partner's child already, do you say to yourself, "He's a nice kid, but I wish he were not so . . ."? Depending on who you are you might be objecting to something very minor, or you may get irritated only when he drinks your bourbon or tortures your dog. Whether the child's behavior has to be endured without hope for change depends on the circumstances and on your, and your partner's, judgment. But you should guard against not saying anything at one extreme, and against continuing to complain all the time at the other. Open up the problem with your partner. Do not be afraid to say to her child, "I just don't like you doing that." It is not being unfair, unkind, or disloyal to speak your mind. It will not harm you to be a little more natural and to try to work out with your partner what the boundaries should be. If you do not take steps to reduce tension before it builds up, then you *are* being unfair, because you are expecting people to understand intuitively what is going wrong.

> I recognize that all children are different, and when my wife's kids started visiting us, well, I was glad they were able to come, and I wasn't going to complain if they weren't what I had expected. They've had a pretty free rein in their house. That's fine. But me—I have an Italian background. We'd never get up halfway through a meal and rush around the house. If my father told me not to let the dog out, I surely did not. Simple as that. Well, these are nice enough kids, don't get me wrong. It's just that they never listened to a word their mother said, or to a word I said. My own son just looked at them bewildered. I put up with this for her sake and for the kids' sake. But sometimes, just sometimes, something out of my background would make me hit the roof. The first time, they had the record player on so loud I couldn't listen to the television in the next room. I asked them very nicely to turn it down. Nothing doing. Their mother asked them very nicely to turn it down. Again, nothing. Then I went crazy. "Don't you ever listen to a word your mother says?" I shouted at them. That was the first time I raised my voice. We'd been seeing each other for a few months by the time this happened. One of the kids cried. Their mother cried. I felt lousy.

Certainly you should make allowances for children having different upbringings and different personalities. But by sitting back and suffering you are not making the house a happy one, you are turning it into a smoldering volcano.

Talk to your partner and to the children. Living together successfully so that you look forward to the next visit requires compromises, not abdication.

When you are meeting your partner's children for the first time and they are over the age of eight, there is a disadvantage to consider. Younger than that, it is fairly easy to share some kind of horseplay with them, whether you are carrying them on your back or burying their legs in sand at the beach. When you play together with some physical contact of this kind, assuming they enjoy it, there is a quicker acceptance of you as an adult who is strong and reliable. They respect you for the fun you provide, and for the fact that you know when to stop using your strength. This helps build trust. But there is no point whatever in playing this way with older children unless they initiate it. If either you or the child is uncomfortable about physical contact, leave it alone.

Having said this, if your partner's child is male and between about ten and fourteen, you may well expect to be jumped on in the swimming pool or subjected to the sudden application of an armlock to see if you can get out of it. It may be painful, but it's usually a good sign. It's a test that somebody becoming a teenager likes to impose on an adult. It may also have an element of showing off in front of his mother, to emphasize his growth and strength and increased ability to look after her if need be. If you can accept this good-naturedly and stand up for yourself, too, your relationship will profit.

Occasionally a girl will try to do the same kind of thing. In self-defense you will probably have to join in. It is most unwise to push her away because she is a girl. But fathers do not normally wrestle with girls in the same way that they do with boys: discuss with your partner what her feelings are on the subject and go by what *she* is comfortable with.

Another type of physical contact that raises problems is demonstrating affection. This seems harder sometimes for a male new partner than for a female. Showing affection to someone, even a young person, whom you do not know all that well seems sometimes more appropriate for a woman than for a man. Should your partner's child look surprised or uncomfortable if you give him or her a hug, this is a warning to stop right there. Don't draw back as if you have blundered—that just ensures that the embarrassment will go on for much longer. Simply stop. Should your partner urge her child to greet you or say good-bye in this way, it is better to take the child's side. Murmur something diplomatic like "I'm not sure you want to right now, do you?" with a smile.

Children in a loyalty crisis may be abruptly reminded of it by sudden affectionate contact with you. They may be having trouble persuading themselves that it is all right to enjoy life with each of their parents and with you as well. Such a child may be happy to give you a kiss on the cheek one week but not the next. You can only guess why. You certainly should not quiz the child about it. Even jokes like "Playing hard-to-get this week, are you?" do not make it easier for him to sort out his feelings.

Comparisons between women tend to be different from comparisons between men. The father's new partner is usually compared to the mother in terms of personality. But the mother's new partner seems more likely to be compared to the father in terms of what each *does* or *has*. You may prefer to be evaluated as a person, and in the end that will probably happen, but at first your partner's child may assess you more on the basis of social status and material possessions.

The conclusions drawn by the child from the evidence before him may be quite different from what you expect. For example, the value put on a desk job earning a hefty salary may be considerably lower than work with animals or machines. Then again, if you have a small personal computer you may acquire far more status in a child's eyes (depending, of course, on the child) than if you own an indoor pool or a sports car. Be prepared to be examined, directly or indirectly, on your salary and the cost of your house. You are not necessarily being spied on by the father (although this has been known to happen). At school, children discuss each other's fathers' wealth, and how they acquire it—this is part of having an identity. In your case the child is making a comparison between two male adults in his life. He is not particularly anxious for either to be "the winner." But he is curious all the same.

For many new male partners the problem in the early months is not so much *how* the child thinks of you as *whether* he ever bothers to think about you at all. Sometimes it is hard to get more than monosyllabic answers. Perhaps, you think, he would prefer it if I just were not there. Occasionally men report that the child seems to get used to everything else in a new house—the rooms, the furniture, the television, the refrigerator—more quickly and easily than he adapts to his mother's new partner. Avoidance games are played, and they are frustrating.

Unresponsiveness has several causes. A younger child may be going through a shy stage. He may have a fear of situations where he might be embarrassed, especially through being found inadequate. You threaten his pride by being strong, different, and less predictable than anyone the child has known so far. Shyness passes when self-confidence increases and you become more predictable. You may be under observation by a shy child for a long time. You may feel ignored, but this is not the case.

Another cause of the cold-shoulder treatment is resentment that you are there at all. Boys more often, but girls, too, sometimes decide that even if they are not always with their mother, it is they who are the logical companions and protectors. You are seen to be competing for that role. Should you incline toward the traditionalist head-of-the-household position, their resentment is likely to increase. The child simply dislikes seeing you exercising authority over his mother. Where there is more give and take, he accepts more naturally and easily the idea of his mother enjoying your company and the image of the two of you supporting each other.

Older children who ignore the new male partner may be swayed by other considerations. They have no wish, perhaps, to confront yet another authority figure (which you are more likely to be, since you are a man). The presence of a new partner in their own home may already have added to their problems of adjustment. Now there is you. Another possibility is that the child has been enjoying singular success at playing off one natural parent against the other: each is unwilling to exert any discipline for fear of losing the child's affection. You present a difficulty because you are not bound by the same emotional rope and he may keep judiciously out of your way.

Then, too, there is embarrassment. A teenager may see in you an obvious example of a male being sexually attracted to a female at an age when adults are supposed by many teenagers to be beyond such things, or at least more settled in their ways. Because you are male, you are seen as the seeker and the finder. The reality does not matter. A teenager's view is usually the traditional one: the male sex pursues and the female sex acquiesces. It is the thought of their mother acquiescing that makes them nervous and antagonistic toward somebody like yourself. It gets worse if their mother, too, is embarrassed in front of them because you are there.

Whatever the cause of the averted eyes, the mumbled answers, and the apologetic refusal when you suggest something that the two of you should do together, you have a tightrope to walk. On the one side, you want to avoid indifference; on the other, you don't want to be seen as a nagging intruder. Keep making friendly approaches, then, but vary them, and don't make them either intense or too frequent.

Indifference on your part is a mistake. It is easy to decide to ignore the child so long as he ignores you. But this suggests to a child that you don't much care for his company; he may decide that perhaps the best solution *is* to continue as if you were not there. Ignoring each other is a bad preparation for taking action in any kind of a crisis. It cannot be much fun for your partner, either, who must have regrets about the change in atmosphere that occurs when her child comes to visit.

However, lowering your head and acting like a battering ram will not do much good, either. For one thing, this seriously eats into the time that mother and child have together. It creates a sense of battle, too. However skillfully you combine various tactics of coaxing and cajoling, the net result of continued attack on the child's private castle is to stiffen resistance. You may get some sense of superficial breakthrough. Exhausted, the child may decide that it is easier to give you a "Good morning," and possibly even "How is your business going?" You can force politeness to a degree, but smiles are harder to extract.

Getting your partner to win the child to your side is not very sensible or effective. If the child is downright rude and unpleasant, his mother should intervene. But she cannot force the pace of friendliness any more than you can. The results will be stilted, and there may be more friction between her and her child than can be handled during a brief visit.

The middle path is to show some interest, some kindness, and some friendliness. Take it easy. Although the time span of any particular visit or vacation is short, you should reflect that you may have a very long time ahead of you for a protracted relationship. The more relaxed you are, the more the child is likely to relax with you, too. When your overture is rebuffed, think up another one.

Eventually the ice will melt, provided that you: keep paying the occasional compliment; keep up a lighthearted approach; ask occasionally about things that you know to be important to the child; suggest little things to do together, from getting a spare part for the car to visiting a pet shop to look at the animals; offer little tokens (no *big* presents) such as magnets, decals, hair barrettes, cake—not by clockwork, but fairly occasionally and on an unpredictable basis; remembering what the individual child likes and dislikes. Even the most sullen teenager will not remain indifferent to repeated acts of kindness, particularly when the kindness also extends to his mother.

Never argue with your partner about the child or the tactics you are adopting with him if the child can overhear. Privately you should by all means discuss your ideas. But if either of you informs him that there is difficulty in creating communication between you and him, the obstacles will grow.

Time will help you. It will give the child a chance to observe how supportive you are of his mother and it will help him compare your behavior with that of his father. It will show him that you have a friendly disposition, and that even though there are times when you have to say "Please don't do that," you have fair rules.

There is a good chance (greater than if you were a new female partner) that you are a Saturday parent yourself. That is, you have your own children living apart from you, whom you see from time to time. This gives you an advantage in that you can sympathize in a more direct way with your partner when things go wrong with arrangements for access. Against this advantage is an obligation to be fair with your partner over the timing of visits and the choices of activities.

Each and every Saturday parent tends to be conscious of problems that arise from changes in a visiting schedule and of the influence exerted by his own child's preference for a particular weekend activity. But if there are two Saturday parents sharing the home, you must make occasional compromises. Sometimes you will want all the children together, sometimes not, depending on their ages, how they get on, and how long it is since they have seen you. When both ex-spouses offer two entirely different visiting schedules, are you going to take separate vacations, or is one of you going to make an attempt to renegotiate? The most important issue is that your compromises are fair to both of you.

As a man, you may have a different perception of the importance of your employment. If this is the case, you are more likely to demand changes in *her* visiting arrangements that let you keep *your* job and perform it well. In one household with two Saturday parents, it was always the woman who had to adjust her visits with her two sons to fit in with the requirements of her new partner's job. He was a salesman who had to take his car full of samples to distant cities every so often, not always at predictable times. This was the only car in the household. When his partner could get her ex-husband to agree to let her children visit on the same weekends as the new partner's, things went easily. But this was unusual. Most of the time she had to use public transportation. She calculated that about one third of the time she had to spend with her children was spent in a bus or waiting for a train. The salesman was very anxious not to jeopardize his business: he earned about twice what his partner earned. But resentment rose until it became a serious issue. When he thought she was being unreasonable in wanting more money to pay for taxi fares, she moved out.

In the two-Saturday-parent situation, the compromises really have to come from both sides. Sometimes this means some hard bargaining, not just with your ex-spouse, but with your child, too. For example, if a promised trip to a baseball game has to be put off because of your partner's arrangements for her child, try to present to your child a positive alternative for what you can do that particular weekend. Avoid making your child feel resentful of your partner and her child. Don't blame it all on them, and remind your child of a compromise they have made that benefits *him*, either in the past or for the future.

Ask your partner from time to time whether she feels that you are being fair and impartial to her children as well as to your own. This seems to be a problem slightly more often when the new partner is a man. Your partner will appreciate the concern that you show in offering to discuss the topic every so often.

Men like yourself seldom seem to regret having given time and help (and sometimes money, too) to their partners so that contact between mother and child could be maintained. They take a justifiable pride in situations where they feel they have helped a child get closer to his mother. This is particularly the case when the child had undergone a stressful period (in general behavior, in poor school progress, or just feeling bad) and was able to develop a more positive and a more likable personality. They don't claim all the credit, but they are proud of a certain contribution. When they have made close friends with the child, they feel another dimension of satisfaction. This, however, depends very much on personal chemistry.

In addition to the obvious variables, such as whether you like each other's looks, mannerisms, ways of talking, and the like, you must contend with the discord between young adults and older adults about how life should be lived. This can arise in any family, however happy. But there are some pressures at work in your own case that may be worth thinking about. For one thing, you may expect the child (as he grows older) to be supportive of his mother. You would prefer him to feel some sense of obligation toward her—for being his mother, for having taken a lot of trouble to maintain contact with him, and for being somebody you love. You know that she cares a great deal about him, and you feel that some obligation is justified in return. But turn this around: if you were a woman, and the child's absent parent were his father, would your feelings about obligation be exactly the same? Possibly; but more likely not. Simply because the concept of an obligation to one's mother seems more basic, new male partners sometimes seem to develop unrealistic expectations. Apart from trying to become an adult and fighting all the battles that that involves, this young person has a complex diplomatic balancing act to perform between two families once it becomes *his* choice as to where to spend Christmas or Thanksgiving. He has not had a "normal" background, so expecting him to have a "normal" sense of obligation and a "normal" way of expressing it is really demanding too much.

The child's father is undoubtedly curious about you and about what influence you might have on his child. Nobody, however fair-minded he might wish to be, really appreciates somebody else exercising a father's influence over his own child. When a father has custody, you may be sure that he feels very strongly about this. If he feels that your star is rising in his child's estimation, he may take some corrective action. Sometimes this may involve a violent act, such as finding out where you live and smashing your windows or attempting to hit you. This is rare but not unknown. It rarely makes the newspapers, and even more rarely requires police intervention (as a "family matter" it tends to be avoided by the police on principle). It is more common by far for the father to ask the child a few questions about you, and make some comment designed to reduce enthusiasm for you. (For the moment you will know very little about this. Years later, you may be told about it by the child when he finds it easier to discuss.) When you get odd questions suddenly thrown at you, including odd assumptions about your life-style, you can guess that some ideas about you may be being put into his mind by his father. Never press a child to tell you more about this, but keep it in mind.

Greg

The younger of Greg's partner's two children, a six-year-old boy, commented that the bathtub in Greg's house was "pink, not purple." Nobody took any notice of this until a day later when the boy moved the wrong piece during a board game. His mother corrected him and said, "Yours is the *green* one!" Jokingly she added, "You're not color blind, are you, Tom? First it's a purple bathtub, then it's a . . ."

"Oh, I just thought 'cause he's Greek," Tom said innocently. Greg noticed that Tom's older sister was signaling him to stop.

The children's father had been told, apparently by the sister, that Greg's surname was Greek. He then made some remarks over the breakfast table about Greeks, including the comment that the bathtub in Greg's house was probably purple because all Greeks made homemade wine. Tom's sister, Nora, correctly interpreted this as a kind of slur, and was anxious to stifle any mention of it.

Greg just noted it in the corner of his mind. There was no point in reacting, although the children's mother was upset. He resolved, however, to give the children *Tales of Ancient Greece* the next time that he read to them before bedtime.

These children are still young. They get on well with Greg. There is never any talk between them about the children's father, or what he says about Greg or the Greeks. Meanwhile, *Tales of Ancient Greece* has captured the children's imaginations.

Finally there is the problem of respect. Several men interviewed were on the whole satisfied with the way things had gone; they were happy when their partners had been made happy and they were fond of the children and enjoyed their company. But they felt that something was missing. This comment sums up one man's feelings about it:

> I would like, just once in a while, to get a little respect. Maybe that's the wrong word. Recognition is better. I've gone along to the high school to help his mother persuade the principal not to throw him out. I've carried him home bleeding when he got into a fight. I've mended his tricycle, his bicycle, and his

motorcycle. I taught him to drive. I paid part of his fees for technical college. He's a good kid, don't get me wrong. But do I ever get any respect? (I mean "recognition.") He'll say hello to me, and even buy me a beer. Fine. But if I disappeared, I'm not sure he'd notice. Just so long as there's still food in the house when he visits, and his mother can lend him some cash so he can upgrade his sound system.

Taking things for granted is a charge that has been leveled at virtually every generation of teenagers and young adults that has ever existed. It is rarely in the nature of young people to show the respect and recognition that adults want. But from the evidence of the interviews, this might be a worse problem when there is no blood relationship. When the man has rescued the mother from a difficult financial situation, the resentment may be stronger, too.

Reminding people of the sacrifices you have made simply drives them away. The best satisfaction you will feel is in having done the right thing. And the best respect you will win may well be self-respect, and the respect of your partner.